AF568106

INSTITUTIONS THAT SHAPED MODERN INDIA

SUPREME COURT

INSTITUTIONS THAT SHAPED MODERN INDIA

SUPREME COURT

Ashok Panda

RUPA

Published by
Rupa Publications India Pvt. Ltd 2021
7/16, Ansari Road, Daryaganj
New Delhi 110002

Sales centres:
Prayagraj Bengaluru Chennai
Hyderabad Jaipur Kathmandu
Calcutta Mumbai

The views and opinions expressed in this book are the author's own and the facts are as reported by him which have been verified to the extent possible, and the publishers are not in any way liable for the same.

P-ISBN: 978-93-90356-88-1
E-ISBN: 978-93-90356-96-6

Fourth impression 2025

10 9 8 7 6 5 4

Printed in India

To the late Justice V.M. Tarkunde, a tireless crusader for civil liberties and human rights in India.
He was my guru, at whose feet I learnt law.

CONTENTS

FOREWORD

The Supreme Court of India is an institution of which every Indian can be legitimately proud. It has enforced the Rule of Law and upheld constitutional values and struck down exercise of arbitrary power. More significantly, it has evolved constitutional rights and freedoms not expressly mentioned in the constitutional guarantees. The right to privacy is one such illustration.

The most striking feature of the Supreme Court has been the evolution of the basic structure doctrine, according to which the power of amendment, however wide and extensive, cannot be utilized to change the basic features of the Constitution. For example, secularism is a basic feature of the Constitution. Parliament cannot by constitutional amendment abrogate it. Again, freedom of religion is also a basic feature. Federalism is another basic feature. These features cannot be abrogated because according to the Supreme Court, the same constitute the basic structure of the Constitution and thus, are beyond the power of amendment.

A fierce controversy erupted after the Supreme Court judgment on its basic structure theory. Critics denounced it as an unwarranted assertion of judicial supremacy over other institutions, namely Parliament and State legislatures.

Attempts by legislatures to exercise the power of amendment to usher in so-called progressive legislation by overriding fundamental rights of the people generated severe thoughts and gradually over a period of time, the fiercest critics of the basic structure doctrine became reconciled to its significance and utility in the day-to-day lives of the people of India. Expansion of the concept of justiciability has been admirably dealt with by the author. Public interest litigation is deftly covered under the head and the Supreme Court judgments in the field have been analysed, explained and commented upon with commendable insight. This is a fine example of erudition with a joy for which the author deserves full praise.

The author of the book, *The Supreme Court* has dealt with this aspect in great detail and with lucidity and thoroughness, and he deserves to be commended for the same. Erudition and sound analysis of the Supreme Court judgments are the hallmark of the book which should find a place in the law libraries of practicing advocates, judges of the Supreme Court and high courts and, if I may say so, the Vice President and the President of India.

Soli J. Sorabjee
Former Attorney General of India

INTRODUCTION

In India the 'Constitution is *suprema lex*, the paramount law of the land and there is no authority, no department or branch of the State which is above or beyond the Constitution or has powers unfettered and unrestricted by the Constitution'[1]. Justice is a concept, so theoretical, philosophical and abstract, that even the most eminent have not been able to satisfactorily define it.

This may be the reason that the motto of the Supreme Court is not of justice, but rather of righteousness.

||यताधर्मस्ततोजयः||

'Where there is righteousness, there is victory.'

The Supreme Court of India is one of the most versatile and dynamic judicial institutions in the world. It carries the burden to ensure and safeguard justice for citizens as well as the public and private institutions of the country. It is the guardian of the Constitution and protects the will of the people. Carrying this burden is no mean feat and this task cannot be carried out without legitimacy and power, the extents of which are

---

[1]*Minerva Mills Ltd. v. Union of India, (1980) 3 SCC 625* at Para 86, page 676

constantly debated. The Supreme Court of India has evolved with time.

The Supreme Court was born out of a Constitution that drew its ideals from, not just our colonizers, but from all parts of the world. Due to this mixed bag of ideals, the extent of the Supreme Court's power, legitimacy and identity were never totally clear; it never came to be defined conclusively. Of course, the Constitution was drawn up meticulously by the Constituent Assembly and it set forth the path and model for achieving an India of tomorrow. However, the Constitution was nothing more than a blueprint. To achieve this constitutional vision, it created three organs for its execution—the Parliament and State Legislatures; the Union and State Governments; and finally the Supreme Court as the arbiter of the federal structure, interpreter of the Constitution and the defender of fundamental rights.

The powers and extent of each institution was clearly and carefully outlined in the Constitution, with one exception. Carefully weaved and embedded into the Constitution was the Supreme Court's endless reservoir of power, because the Supreme Court, as it would soon come to find out, was vested with an additional and perhaps, the most important responsibility—to interpret, preserve and protect the Constitution itself. The Supreme Court cannot discharge this Herculean responsibility without being equipped with Herculean power. Thus, the power of the Supreme Court was designated to be supreme in terms of the interpretation of the Constitution. The experience gained by the Supreme Court over a span of seven decades has led the Court to choose its own path and discover the extent of its own capabilities.

The following extracts from the speeches delivered on the inaugural function of the Supreme Court on 28 January 1950, reflect the mood of the time as well as the inherent discordance in the perceptions of jurists, in contrast to those of the political leaders.

M.C. Setalvad, the first Attorney General for India, said[2]:

> 'Your foremost task will be to interpret the Constitution which is but a means of ordering the life of a progressive people. The Federal Court has already laid down that a Constitution is to be interpreted in no narrow spirit.'

The first Chief Justice of India, Sir Harilal J. Kania said[3]:

> 'The duty of interpreting the Constitution with an enlightened liberality falls on the Supreme Court... It will be our endeavor to interpret the Constitution, not as a rigid body, but, as a living organism, having within itself the force and power of self-government...'

However, the political leaders, including Pandit Jawaharlal Nehru, came out with sentiments advocating limited judicial power in contrast to the sovereign power of the legislature.

Pandit Nehru, the first prime minister of the country, said[4]:

> 'No Supreme Court and no judiciary can stand in judgment over the sovereign will of Parliament representing the will of the entire community. If we go

---

[2]Justice R.C. Lahoti, *Canons of Judicial Ethics* (1st Edition, Universal Law Publishing Co., 2005, Delhi), p. 65-66

[3]Ibid., p. 69

[4]Gobind Das, *Supreme Court in Quest of Identity* (2nd Edition, Eastern Book Company, 2000, Lucknow), p. 8

> wrong here and there it can point it out [to us], but in the ultimate analysis, where the future of the community is concerned, no judiciary can come in the way. And if it comes in the way, ultimately, the whole Constitution is a creature of Parliament... But it is obvious that no Court, no system of judiciary can function in the nature of Third House, as a kind of Third House of correction. So, it is important that with this limitation the judiciary should function.'

Dr B.R. Ambedkar, the first Law Minister of independent India, also held a similar view. He said[5]:

> 'I do not see how five or six gentlemen, sitting in the Federal or Supreme Court, examining laws made by the Legislature and by the dint of their own individual conscience or their bias or their prejudice be trusted to determine which law is good and which law is bad.'

Despite specific provisions for appointment of judges under the Constitution, to ensure for an independent judiciary and judicial review under Articles 32, 136, 141 and 142, the political leadership did not wish to concede the power of judicial review and did not want to be made answerable to any authority for its legislative functions. The controversy continues till date and the debate on the dynamics of the Supreme Court's power occupies the national discourse.

Over the course of time, judicial power has grown. Drawing from a Constitution that has provided for a high level of judicial independence, the Supreme Court has passed judgments

[5]Ibid., p. 9

that have expanded and widened both the procedural and substantive powers of the Court—barring the times of political turbulence during the internal Emergency of 1975.

The extensive support of the free media that espouses the cause of public interest and transparency in administrative affairs have, to a great extent, played a critical role in enhancing public respect for the institution. Simultaneously, the courts have espoused freedom of expression and thereby allowed the media to become the fourth pillar of democracy.

Another critical theme is that of the legitimacy of judicial activism. This is a more fiercely debated issue, as it entails impinging on domains of the Legislature and the Executive. Issues of legitimacy have arisen from time to time. The Supreme Court, in the first two decades, was engaged in seeking its identity and understanding its limits in the context of separation of powers. In the third decade, the dark days of Emergency had brought the institution to its knees, creating a general sense of helplessness in the country. Internal and external aggressions created volatility in law and order and caused supersessions in the appointment of the Chief Justice of India on two separate occasions.

As the dark clouds of Emergency passed, the Supreme Court began to assert its presence by evolving the concept of Public Interest Litigation (PIL). The Supreme Court worked tirelessly towards protecting Human Rights and, through directions to the Executive, improving the general living conditions of the marginalized in the country. This marked the start of judicial activism and scrutiny into all forms of questionable legislative and executive action. The Supreme Court took a strong stand against executive inaction and apathy, triggering the Parliament to also become active in the upliftment of the lower strata of Indian society by passing numerous social welfare legislations, seeds of all of which, are embedded in the Constitution. The concentrated efforts of the Supreme Court allowed India to enter the new millennium as a country where human atrocities, crime, corruption, political and governmental instability were in decline. Today, the Supreme Court holds a place of pride for the nation, and has been influential in countering regressive societal thought. Indian societal thought and condition have made considerable progress and now compete with the so-called First World western societies.

One thing that should be borne in mind is that while certain judgments of the Supreme Court do set forth the law, it may not always be good law. But, the facts and circumstances of each case do play an important role in the manner in which the law is developed by the Court. As it is often said, hard cases make for bad law. Each case has with it a contextual narrative to the events; hence, the focus of the courts on various issues also changes with time.

In the life of our nation, preserving the values underpinning the Constitution is the most precious duty that attains utmost importance. It comes as no surprise that any institution tasked with such a mighty burden would find itself facing impossible odds. Such is the experience of the Supreme Court of India.

Challenges that place our institutions in peril have been regular features in the functioning of the Supreme Court since the commencement of the Republic. Constitutional amendments were hastily enacted whenever the Supreme Court made politically disagreeable pronouncements. Despite these complications, the Supreme Court has always held its head high and regularly delivered landmark judgments with far-ranging consequences that would ensure radical changes in the country.

This active involvement in overtly shaping national governance continues to this day, where judgments like Ayodhya and Sabarimala have assumed critical significance. These proceedings have brought issues of secularism, religious freedom, and fundamentalism to the forefront, especially in the light of contemporary political rhetoric and policy decisions.

In Ayodhya, the century-long dispute over whether the Babri Masjid was built on the ruins of a temple that was believed to be the birthplace of Lord Ram, has attained finality with the judgment by the Supreme Court. The judgment set aside the 2010 Allahabad High Court verdict ordering a trifurcation of the disputed land measuring 2.77 acres. The Supreme Court finally held that the entire disputed land be allotted to a Trust, which will construct a temple dedicated to Lord Ram. Simultaneously, the Court characterized 'the destruction of the mosque and the obliteration of the Islamic structure was an egregious violation of the rule of law'. Consequently, the Court, while exercising its constitutional power under Article 142 in order to do complete justice, directed allotment of 5 acres of land at an appropriate place for the construction of a mosque. Divergent views have been expressed by jurists and historians—some criticizing the judgment as being political, and others holding that the Supreme Court was moved by a desire for a pragmatic and equitable solution[6].

---

[6]https://indianexpress.com/article/opinion/columns/ayodhya-verdict-babri-masjid-demolition-supreme-court-ram-temple-6135272/ accessed on 12 December 2019

Eminent personalities such as Prof. Romila Thapar and former Supreme Court Justice A.K. Ganguly have opined that the Ayodhya issues seem to have been dealt by the Supreme Court in a manner that lacks tenor and substance.

Prof. Romila Thapar[7] views the judgment as political, where the Court has annulled respect for history and seeks to replace the same with religious faith. Similarly, noted jurist and former Supreme Court Judge A.K. Ganguly[8], has observed that the conclusions which the Court arrived at, were not matched by its reasons, and that the Court had placed a premium on the blatantly illegal destruction of the mosque.

Thus, for certain segments of the public, it may appear that concerns of decorum, stability and the ease of governance are becoming substantial considerations in judgments, especially when contrasted with the essentials of law and justice.

On the other end, the Ayodhya verdict has also been hailed as an example of an independent Supreme Court delivering justice as it was always meant to do. For example, Soli Sorabjee, former Attorney General of India, well known for his pro-human rights and civil liberties work, has termed the judgment as 'balanced and sensible'[9].

On a similar note, in a 2018 judgment, in Sabarimala, the Supreme Court, by a 4:1 majority, struck down the centuries-old practice of the Sabarimala Temple banning the entry of

---

[7]Renunciation, Dissent and Satyagraha: Prof. Romila Thapar | Tarkunde Memorial Lecture, https://www.youtube.com/watch?v=bmIyyH-aWKQ, accessed on 12 December 2019

[8]https://thewire.in/law/babri-masjid-ayodhya-verdict-justice-ak-ganguly accessed on 12 December 2019

[9]https://www.bloombergquint.com/opinion/supreme-court-ayodhya-verdict-top-lawyers-take-bqdebates accessed on 12 December 2019

women of menstruating age (between 10 to 50 years) on the grounds that the said practice was discriminatory and unconstitutional. While the judgment was widely hailed as path-breaking and progressive for upholding gender-equality and dignity of women, several factions in the country, including the ruling establishment, criticized the same for infringing on religious freedom. Surprisingly, a little more than a year later, the Supreme Court by a 3:2 majority has decided to revisit this judgment, observing that certain issues regarding women rights and religion, such as female genital mutilation in the Dawoodi Bohra community and the marriage of Parsi women and non-Parsi men at the holy fire-place of an Agyari, are yet to be decided. The review petition has been kept open and pending. Though the Court has explicitly emphasized that there was no stay of the Sabarimala judgment, the State Government has openly refused to implement the directions of the Court. This has again turned the clock back with regard to the issue of gender justice.

As the final avenue for justice in the country, the Supreme Court has the unenviable task of keeping its doors open for litigants no matter what the state of the nation. Numerous economic crises, political shifts, wars and civil unrest have shaken the foundations of the nation, but the Supreme Court has muscled through it all, cognizant of its importance in keeping together the constitutional fabric. The Court now faced a new crisis—the COVID-19 pandemic. This crisis has no doubt affected the functioning of the Supreme Court. However, the crisis has become a catalyst for technological advancement in terms of e-filing and video-conferencing through virtual courts. Though the infrastructural support for such technological advancement is deficient in many respects and virtual courts cannot replace the real courts, to a large extent the cause of justice has yet, been preserved. However, the entire judicial system in the country has suffered greatly, especially the criminal justice system. But there is a silver lining of hope that the crisis will finally result in a better and more efficient judicial institution.

Needless to say, the Supreme Court has weathered through turbulent times and today, stands as an institution that garners the trust, respect and faith of people the world over.

However, to understand the social jurisprudence that the Supreme Court has developed over time, we must necessarily begin from the times of British Colonial Rule, as it was from the ashes of these erstwhile systems that the Supreme Court arose—like a phoenix.

1
THE BRITISH RULE AND COLONIAL INDIA

Great Britain set its footprint in India through the East India Company. In 1612, the Mughal Emperor Jahangir allowed the Company to establish a factory in Surat and carry on trade. The success of the first factory fuelled the Company to establish another factory along the south-eastern coast of Madras in 1640. Around this time, the island of Bombay was under the dominion of the Portuguese and was used primarily as an outpost. England gained control over Bombay when it was gifted to them in 1661 by the Portuguese in the marriage treaty between Catherine of Braganza and Charles II of England. Shortly thereafter, the island was leased to the Company by the Crown in 1668.

The formalized structure of the present-day Indian legal system has been largely influenced by the British Common Law. The permeation of the British administration was neither instantaneous nor sweeping, but through a process of gradual evolution.

The administration of British Law in India was confined to the presidency towns of Bombay, Calcutta and Madras. The rest of British-administered India was left to be governed as per the law derived from the prevailing religions and customs.

The advancement, development and modernization of society is closely linked with the efficacy of the legal framework of a nation, and the extent to which it can incubate societal progression. The Crown as well as the British Parliament were not oblivious to this fact, and seeing that the East India Company was consolidating power and control over India, the colonial rulers began the process of formalizing law for India. A major landmark in restructuring the Indian legal system was the codification of laws. India's vast territories contained a myriad of scattered laws, developed over millennia, making the administration of justice difficult and thereby stunting commercial growth. With a lack of uniformity in the application of law, the justice delivery system gave impressions of uncertainty, opacity and ambiguity. The administrators of justice were also burdened by these factors. The prevailing system not only caused difficulties in India, but also for Britain. The pioneers propounding the codification had experientially come to learn that British administration over India could no longer be sustainable or feasible without judicial and legislative reforms in India.

Hence, the first Law Commission was established by the Charter Act of 1833, with Lord Thomas Babington Macaulay as the first Law Commissioner in 1835.

Through the successive law commissions covering the period from 1835 till the beginning of the twentieth century, the process of the codification of laws was undertaken and several statutes brought into force. Some of the major statutes include:

- 1859—Code of Civil Procedure & Law of Limitation (Revised in 1877, 1882 & 1908)
- 1860—Indian Penal Code
- 1861—Code of Criminal Procedure (Revised in 1872)
- 1866—Indian Companies Act
- 1866—Trustees Act
- 1868—General Clauses Act
- 1869—Divorce Act
- 1870—Court Fees Act
- 1870—Land Acquisition Act
- 1872—Indian Contract Act
- 1872—Indian Evidence Act
- 1872—Special Marriages Act
- 1881—Negotiable Instruments Act
- 1882—Transfer of Property Act
- 1882—Indian Trusts Act

Even today, these statutes cover the near majority of litigation in the country. However, the personal laws of different communities remained untouched and were left to be governed by their respective customs and usages.

The second landmark development of the Indian legal system was the establishment of the high courts in India. The Second Law Commission, created under the Charter Act of 1853, had devised the model for the creation of the high courts by amalgamating the Supreme Courts and Sadar Diwani Adalats. This harmonized well with the system of the codification of laws. Accepting the recommendations of the Law Commission, the British Parliament established high courts of Madras, Bombay and Calcutta in 1861. Thereafter, the High Court of Allahabad and the Chief Court of Punjab were both established in 1866.

The Courts established by the Charter still continue today in independent India.

2

INDIA'S MARCH TOWARDS SELF-RULE

Solon, the Athenian lawmaker and one of the seven wise men of ancient Greece was asked,

'Which is the best city to live in?'

> 'That city,' he replied, 'in which those who are not wronged, no less than those who are wronged, exert themselves to punish the wrongdoers.'[1]

The freedom struggle in India picked up momentum after the first world war. Indians were very hopeful that the British colonial rulers would reward India for its sacrifice and support to the British war efforts, wherein about 14 lakh Indian soldiers fought under the British flag. More than 74 thousand soldiers laid down their lives and several lakhs returned home injured. To the utter dismay of Indians, the British colonial power enacted the Government of India Act of 1919, which was a far cry from the promises of autonomy and self-rule. Adding insult to injury, the Anarchical and Revolutionary Crimes Act of 1919, infamously known as the Rowlatt Act, was simultaneously

---

[1]http://penelope.uchicago.edu/Thayer/E/Roman/Texts/Plutarch/Lives/Solon*.html (accessed on 5 July 2019)

introduced, to put an end to any illusion of attaining self-rule. India, in the twenties and thirties, was witness to the most horrific acts of colonial repression, the most notorious being the Jallianwala Bagh massacre.

Despite these oppressive measures, the freedom struggle gained momentum in the form of the non-cooperation movement led by the Indian National Congress. Owing to these concentrated efforts, the British were slowly losing control over the administration in India. The Simon Commission, composed of only British members, was a feeble attempt to assuage the popular resentment and was rejected across the country. After three successive Round Table Conferences which saw the participation of leaders representing different segments of Indian society—the Indian National Congress, the Muslim League, and the princely states—the colonial administration brought about the Government of India Act, 1935 as the final concerted effort for governing British India. The Act of 1935 articulated three major goals: establishing a federal structure, granting provincial autonomy, and safeguarding minority interests through separate electorates. The Act made it compulsory for the provinces of British India to join the proposed federation, whereas, for the princely states, membership into the federation was voluntary. The Act established a bicameral legislature in the form of the Council of States (upper house) and the Central Legislative Assembly (lower house). Members from the provinces were to be elected, while the representatives from the princely states were to be nominated by their respective rulers. Members to the Provincial Legislature were to be elected on the basis of limited franchise, which prescribed minimum income and property ownership criteria. Thus, only around 14 per cent of the population in British India was eligible to participate in the electoral process.

Under the Government of India Act of 1935, powers of the Legislature were severely restricted with the British-appointed governors having extensive discretionary powers. The Central Legislature also had no control over defence and foreign relations. The Act of 1935 provided for three legislative lists enumerating matters on which the federal government and the provincial governments had exclusive power to legislate. It also provided for a concurrent list comprising matters over which both governments could legislate and in case of 'repugnancy' between their laws on the same subject, the federal law was to prevail. The Constituent Assembly adopted this scheme of distribution of powers between the Union and the States into the Constitution of India, although with certain modifications, in view of the object of having a strong Centre.

In exercise of the provisions of the Act of 1935, the Federal Court was established in 1937, vested with jurisdiction to adjudicate inter-state disputes and matters concerning the interpretation of the Government of India Act. It was not, however, the final court of appeal and the British Privy Council remained the apex court.

Thus, with the Government of India Act, India became familiar with the American doctrine of judicial umpiring—resolution of disputes between the Centre and the states and limiting each to confines of their legislative competencies. Important decisions were given by the high courts, the Federal Courts and the Privy Council on the validity of legislation passed by the Federal and provincial governments under the Government of India Act, 1935. Several of these judgments continue to serve as precedents with regard to Centre–state relations under our present Constitution.

3
THE CONSTITUENT ASSEMBLY

The call for a Constitution to be framed by Indians and for India was made by the All Party Conference held in May, 1928 at Lucknow. This led to the formation of the Nehru Committee of 1928. The Committee, after thorough deliberations, came out with the basic features of a Constitution; which was influenced by the American Bill of Rights and the doctrine of Separation of Powers. Along with Pandit Motilal Nehru, the report, also known as the Nehru Report, was finally signed by political luminaries like Sir Tej Bahadur Sapru, Netaji Subhas Chandra Bose, Sir Ali Imam, Dr Madhav Shrihari Aney, Mangal Singh, Shuaib Qureshi and G.R. Pradhan.

The genesis of the Nehru Report could also be traced to the following prophetic sentiment expressed by Mahatma Gandhi in the year 1922:

> 'Let us see clearly what Swaraj, together with the British connection, means. It means undoubtedly India's ability to declare her independence if she wishes. Swaraj therefore, will not be a free gift of the British Parliament. It will be a declaration of India's full expression. That it will be expressed through an Act

> of Parliament is true. But it will be merely a courteous ratification of the declared wish of the people of India, even as it was in the case of the Union of South Africa. Not an unnecessary adverb could be altered by the House of Commons. The ratification in our case will be a treaty to which Britain will be a party. Such Swaraj may not come this year, may not come within our own generation. But I have contemplated nothing less. The British Parliament, when the settlement comes, will ratify the wishes of the people of India as expressed not through the bureaucracy but through her freely chosen representatives.'[2]

The Indian National Congress formally demanded the formation of a constituent assembly composed of representative Indians who could be trusted to express the will of the people of India. Reacting to the proposals contained in the White Paper issued by the Government of India in 1933 which is also known as the proposals for Indian Constitutional Reform of 1933, the Congress Working Committee in June 1934 came out with the following declaration which was reaffirmed several times from 1937 onwards:

> 'The only satisfactory alternative to the White Paper is a constitution drawn up by a Constituent Assembly elected on the basis of adult franchise or as near it as possible, with the power, if necessary, to the important minorities to have their representatives

[2]Quoted in: Gurmukh Nihal Singh, *The Idea of an Indian Constituent Assembly*, published in the Indian Journal of Political Science Vol. 2, No. 3 (January—March 1941), pp. 255–256

elected exclusively by the electors belonging to such minorities.'[3]

The Constituent Assembly owes its origin to the May 1946 negotiations between the Indian leaders and the Cabinet Mission composed of Lord Pethick-Lawrence, the Secretary of State for India and Sir Stafford Cripps.

The Constituent Assembly, though formed by indirect election, with its members having limited representation, was perhaps the best collection of the entire intellectual leadership of the country. The Assembly included stalwarts like Pandit Jawaharlal Nehru, Sardar Vallabhbhai Patel, C. Rajagopalachari, Maulana Abul Kalam Azad, Dr Rajendra Prasad, Sarat Chandra Bose, K.M. Munshi, Dr B.R. Ambedkar, Babu Jagjivan Ram, Syama Prasad Mukherjee, Pandit Govind Ballabh Pant, Rajkumari Amrit Kaur, Acharya J.B. Kripalani, Mrs Hansa Mehta, Sardar K.M. Panikkar and T.T. Krishnamachari, among many other notable and brilliant minds.

The Assembly constituted a number of Committees like the Drafting Committee, with Dr B.R. Ambedkar as the chairman and the Advisory Committee with Sardar Vallabhbhai Patel as the chairman. The Advisory Committee was further divided into sub-committees like the fundamental rights Sub-Committee, Minority Rights Sub-Committee, etc.

The Objectives Resolution passed on 13 December 1946, was a major milestone in structuring the path the Assembly would follow in drafting the Constitution. Pandit Jawaharlal

[3]Quoted in: K.P. Singh, *'Role of the Congress in the Framing of India's Constitution'* published in the Indian Journal of Political Science Vol. 51, No. 2 (April—June 1990), p. 155

Nehru introduced the Objectives Resolution, and opened with the bold and firm resolve 'to proclaim India as an Independent Sovereign Republic and to draw up for her future governance a Constitution'[4].

It was resolved[5], amongst others, that:

> 'Wherein all power and authority of the Sovereign Independent India, its constituent parts and organs of government, are derived from the people;
>
> Wherein it shall be guaranteed and secured to all the people of India justice, social, economic and political: equality of status, of opportunity, and before the law; freedom of thought, expression, belief, faith, worship, vocation, association and action, subject to law and public morality.'

The Congress's desire to move forward in its journey to independent India was best epitomized by Pandit Jawaharlal Nehru before the All India Congress Committee which met at Delhi on 5 January 1947, when he stated:

> 'We have gone through the valley of shadows and we will go through it again for true independence.'[6]

However, with India attaining independence on 15 August

---

[4]Constituent Assembly Debates (CAD), https://www.constitutionofindia.net/constitution_assembly_debates/volume/1/1946-12-13 (accessed on 5 July 2019)

[5]CAD, https://www.constitutionofindia.net/constitution_assembly_debates/volume/1/1946-12-13 (accessed on 5 July 2019)

[6]Quoted in: Vineeta Shekhawat and Vibhuti Shekhawat, *'Indian Constitution Model Designing and Summation'* published in the Indian Journal of Political Science Vol. 51, No. 1 (January–March, 1990), p. 60

1947, the entire landscape of the Constituent Assembly and its status dramatically changed. The Constituent Assembly now stood in its sovereign glory.

While the greatest of minds were basking in the euphoria of making India's freedom a reality and laying the foundation that would guide India through her independent life, the reality on the ground was starkly opposite. The impending partition along the communal lines was looming ominously. Communal passion was being aroused throughout the country leading to violence of catastrophic proportions.

4

BUILDING THE NEW JUDICIAL PARADIGM

The Constitution of India was framed by the Constituent Assembly which first met on 9 December 1946 and continued till 24 January 1950. The Constitution was adopted and enacted in the Constituent Assembly on 26 November 1949 and it came into effect on 26 January 1950. Article 124 of the Constitution of India established the Supreme Court of India and provided that there shall be a Supreme Court of India consisting of a Chief Justice of India and other judges.

The independence of India was the culmination of a long and hard struggle, and the aspirations of the people of India who had freed themselves from the yoke of foreign rule were reflected in the constitutional document. The principles of fundamental rights, independence of judiciary and judicial review were paramount in the minds of the framers of the Constitution and mark their stamp throughout the Constitution. The framing of the Constitution was a watershed moment. The Constitution was to be the compass and rudder of the nation's voyage and at the same time its anchor. The Supreme Court had a very special place in the heart and mind of the Constituent

Assembly. The Supreme Court was not envisaged as just another institution or only a court at the apex, but was seen to be champion of democracy, defender of the citizens' rights and liberties, and interpreter and protector of the Constitution. With the Constitution framed and drawn, the nation had begun its voyage. But this voyage was not to be of any one or two generations, but for countless generations to come. The Supreme Court was to guide the nation by interpreting the law and the Constitution, to defend the people and their precious rights, and to keep the executive and legislative arms of the State within their legitimate arena. The Supreme Court was supreme not because it was at the apex of the hierarchy of courts but because it was to be supreme to the fate of the nation.

The Constitution being a culmination of the freedom struggle, naturally a great emphasis was placed on the fundamental rights. Having experienced disabilities and repression at the hands of the foreign masters, the framers were determined to accord, to certain rights, the status of fundamental rights in the Constitution, which would form a check on the powers of the State. The rights of the people and citizens were accorded a special status in the Constitution and the framers provided a complete chapter in the Constitution dedicated to fundamental rights. These fundamental rights, embodied in Part III, form the bedrock of the Constitution. However, the framers understood that without remedies there are no fundamental rights and thus provided the right to enforcement of the fundamental rights through the Supreme Court and the high courts, under Article 32 and Article 226 respectively. The Supreme Court occupied a special place in the minds of the framers during the debates and was on several occasions referred to as 'the soul of democracy'[7] and 'the supreme guardian of the citizens' rights in any democracy'[8]. The framers made it a point to provide that a common man could move the highest court of the country for the enforcement of his or her fundamental rights. It was important for this right to move the highest court to itself be made a fundamental right. Although there was provision for enforcement of the fundamental rights through the high courts as well, the Supreme Court as the highest court of the land was to be 'the biggest champion of the liberties of our people'[9]. The Supreme Court was not meant to be a mere institution at the apex of the judicial system but was meant to be the guardian of the rights, accessible by the common man.

The scheme of the Constitution provided for a federal structure comprising the union and the states. The Constitution set the parameters for the functioning of the executive and the legislature—both at the central and state levels. A federal structure allowed the sphere of the union and state executives to be clearly defined. The sphere of Parliament and the state legislature was similarly defined. In a federal set-up, judicial review was necessary. It was the role of the judiciary to determine whether the executives and the legislatures at the Centre and the states were working within the set parameters of the Constitution or were usurping powers beyond their scope. In a federal set-up there could be occasions of disputes arising between the central executive and a state executive and among

---

[7]Constituent Assembly Debates (CAD), Vol. VII, p.940
[8]CAD, Vol. VII, p.940
[9]CAD, Vol. VII, p.945

state executives. Therefore, the framers bestowed the Supreme Court with the role of being the arbiter of such disputes.

The structure of the executive and legislature was federal in nature. This means that the Constitution provided for a Central government with distinct governments in the States, as well as a Parliament to frame laws for the entire country and the state legislatures to frame laws for their respective states. However, there was a marked tilt towards the Centre and comparatively more powers were conferred upon the Union executive and the Parliament. This decision was consciously undertaken as the nation was nascent and independence had come with the trauma of partition and the stress of unification of various erstwhile princely states into the Union. Insofar as the judiciary is concerned, the framers refrained from having a dual system akin to the United States of America, where there is a dual court system—one for federal law and another for state law. The framers of our constitution adopted a unitary model, which consisted of a single hierarchy of courts with the Supreme Court at the apex. The high courts in the states would deal with both the central and state executive as well as laws framed by both the Parliament and the state legislatures. The Supreme Court was placed at the top of the pyramid.

5
JURISDICTION

Practically, there are no limits to the jurisdiction of the Supreme Court in India. The Constitution has conferred a wide array of jurisdictions, and a composite analysis of these jurisdictions and powers clearly show the versatility of the Supreme Court's jurisdiction. Therefore, what is more interesting, is the manner in which the Supreme Court exercises its jurisdiction and its discretion in entertaining matters of varying nature and degrees of importance.

The framers of the Constitution envisaged a Supreme Court with wide powers unparalleled to any other country in the world. The Constitution confers various jurisdictions to the Supreme Court: original—in disputes between states and between states and the Centre, appellate—in both civil and criminal matters, in matters of interpretation of the Constitution, and for enforcement of fundamental rights. Besides these, a vast jurisdiction has been granted under Article 136, to the Supreme Court, in the form of a discretionary grant of special leave, to appeal from any judgment, decree, determination, sentence or order, in any cause or matter, passed or made by any court or tribunal in the territory of India. The framers deliberately worded this jurisdiction in the widest possible language. One member emphasized the importance of this jurisdiction in the Constitution and remarked, 'If there is a Supreme Court, it will have to have supreme powers'[10]. Another member stated that this Article laid down one important principle of the constitution, that, while in the scheme of the Government of India Act 1935, the executive was all powerful and both the legislature and the judiciary were subordinate to it, this Article had given a status to the judiciary equivalent and was in no way subordinate to the executive and the legislature.[11] Another member remarked that the jurisdiction of this Article was 'almost divine in nature' for the Supreme Court would do complete justice between States and persons before it.[12]

The framers of the Constitution were anxious to ensure that the judiciary was absolutely independent of the executive. This was particularly necessary, as during British rule, the country had witnessed powers of the judiciary and the executive vested in the same officer, especially at the level of the magistrate who functioned as both, judge and administrator. Throughout the debates in the Constituent Assembly, while discussing fundamental rights, directive principles of state policy and the three organs of the state, one cannot help but notice the recurrent theme of an independent judiciary—free from the influence of the executive and the legislature.

The jurisdiction of the Supreme Court has been set forth under Articles 131 to 143 of the Constitution. Apart from the Constitution, certain special statutes like the Customs Act, 1962; the Advocates Act, 1961; the Competition Act, 2002; the Contempt of Courts Act, 1971; the Income Tax Act, 1961; etc.

---

[10]Constituent Assembly Debates (CAD), Vol. VIII, p.636
[11]CAD, Vol. VIII, p.637
[12]CAD Vol. VIII p.638

provide for statutory appeals to the Supreme Court, arising out of proceedings under such special statutes.

The Court's exercise of jurisdiction presently shows that it has become more of an appellate court than a constitutional court. The purpose inherent in this is to lay down the principles, so that matters, similar in kind, can be settled in the lower courts as well. Although it is with good intent that, at times, there are no principles being settled, and more so at best, are being reaffirmed in the appeal. While criteria for admission of matters under the Special Leave Jurisdiction prescribed under Article 136 is quite strict, it is also discretionary, and over the course of time, its interpretation seems to have evolved. However, the admission rate of matters under Special Leave Jurisdiction could also be an indicator of the Supreme Court's trust in the validity of orders passed by the lower courts.

6

STRUGGLE FOR SUPREMACY

The foundation of law in independent India emanates from the preamble to the Constitution of India. It signifies that the people of India have come together to form themselves in a Sovereign Democratic Republic and have bound themselves to the Rule of Law lensed through the Constitution. After deep deliberation, the preamble, capturing the values for and of India, stood to read:

> 'WE, THE PEOPLE OF INDIA, having solemnly resolved to constitute India into a SOVEREIGN DEMOCRATIC REPUBLIC and to secure to all its citizens:
>
> JUSTICE, social, economic and political;
>
> LIBERTY of thought, expression, belief, faith and worship;
>
> EQUALITY of status and of opportunity; and to promote among them all
>
> FRATERNITY assuring the dignity of the individual and the unity of the Nation;
>
> IN OUR CONSTITUENT ASSEMBLY this twenty-sixth day of November, 1949, do HEREBY ADOPT,

ENACT AND GIVE TO OURSELVES THIS CONSTITUTION.'

The struggle for supremacy between the executive and the judiciary has been long-drawn and spanned over several decades. It was an inevitable battle borne from the Constitution itself. The cold windy day of 28 January 1950 quite beautifully reflected the mood of the Supreme Court inauguration. The government of the day, led by Pandit Jawaharlal Nehru, did not want the Supreme Court impeding the execution of its vision for India. The judiciary, on the other hand, knew that their role was to stop the other competing wings of the State from acting beyond constitutional limits in framing laws and executing policies.

Upon being cloaked with judicial authority, their allegiance shifted from their brothers in the fight for freedom to the newly formed Constitution—to protect its letter and spirit. Naturally, therefore, in the undercurrents of the new nation, the fight for supremacy had begun. The winner would hold charge and custody of the Constitution.

The Nehru-led government quickly became aware of the challenges in maintaining unbridled control under the Constitution. The government improved its public support through the abolition of zamindari and acquisition of private lands for public use, which although was seen as tyrannical by the affected landowners, was widely welcomed by the mass public, boosting the support for the ruling Congress Party. The government acquired lands and awarded paltry sums of money to the landowners as compensation. These actions came under challenge in *State of West Bengal vs Mrs Bela Banerjee*

(AIR 1954 SC 170), and the Supreme Court was tasked with interpreting the term 'compensation' under Article 31 of the Constitution. The government argued that as land acquisition was being effected for public benefit and welfare, it did not warrant an award of market-value compensation. However, holding against the government, the Supreme Court gave an interpretation of 'fair equivalent value', thereby granting landowners market value compensation. It was by this judgment that the ruling party began to perceive the Court as a threat to its supremacy.

The Congress Party, having absolute majority in the Parliament and in command of the government, believed itself to be fit to decide the future of the nation, and believed itself to be the commander of the Constitution. Its reign had to be unfettered, and rather than conforming to the constitutional mandate, it pressed the courts for an interpretation that moulded in favour of its legislative and executive actions.

Thus began a series of surgical attacks that ultimately led to the development of regressive, oppressive and unnatural constitutional law. The incumbent adopted a two-fold approach for achieving their goal—first, through executive action, to restrict personal liberty and human rights in order to oppress dissenting voices and thereby dominate the elections and maintain power, and second, by establishing parenthood and dominion over the Constitution itself through legislative action.

History bore witness to degradation of law over the course of three decades and Indians first-hand saw how absolute power corrupted absolutely, and in despondent hindsight as we tread from the *A.K. Gopalan* case to *Maneka Gandhi*, we will come to realize why the framers of the Constitution had so intensively laboured to separate powers and attempted to make the Constitution itself supreme, and furthermore realize the importance of the judiciary in safeguarding the constitutional ideals from denigration.

7
PERSONAL LIBERTY

The development, evolution and protection of human rights through judicial intervention hinges around the Supreme Court's interpretation of Article 21 of the Constitution. Perhaps no other Article in the Constitution as attracted as much attention, controversy and deliberation as Article 21. Even in the Constituent Assembly, this Article underwent several changes, until it finally stood to read as:

> 'Article 21. Protection of Life and Liberty—No person shall be deprived of his life or personal liberty *except according to procedure established by law*'.

It was initially contemplated to incorporate the 'due process of law' clause from the United States Constitution as the fetter to the right guaranteed under this Article. With this in mind, India's constitutional advisor—Sir B.N. Rau, met with Justice Frankfurter of the US Supreme Court for his views. This historic meeting changed the course of human rights development in India. Justice Frankfurter opined that judicial review, as implicit in the 'due process' clause, would weigh down the Constitutional Courts heavily. Justice Frankfurter, at that moment, was very bothered by competing interpretations to the 'due process' clause under the US Constitution and he did not like the idea of the Indian Constitutional Courts encountering similar controversies. Finally, the Constituent Assembly was persuaded to drop the 'due process' clause, by replacing it with 'procedure established by law'.

With this, the development of the right to personal liberty was left to the Indian Constitutional Courts. As a corollary, the Supreme Court was tasked to interpret the 'procedure established by law' fetter to Article 21 in a manner that would fit the political, economic, social and cultural contours of India, without being unduly pressed by the interpretation of the American 'due process' clause. The constitutional courts of independent India had to assess their own place and determine the extent of their intervention in the will of the legislature and the executive. As history would have it, this exercise would take nearly three decades.

But the burden placed on the judiciary in interpreting this Article cannot be overlooked. A holistic examination of this Article would reveal that no other provision in the Constitution is more fluid than or as vast as Article 21. This Article evolved with the social and cultural progress of this country and has been wielded as a sword as well as a shield. It is independent India's peculiar history that has allowed the Supreme Court to establish the supremacy of Article 21 over the course of time. Indeed, Article 21 still stands as it is, without amendment.

8

LIBERTY

Article 21 was the centerpiece to structuring the development of the country, and thus, the Constituent Assembly thought it wise to leave its interpretation open to free India.

During the period from the case of *A.K. Gopalan* to the case of *Maneka Gandhi*, the executive and legislature, both controlled by the Congress Party enjoying absolute majority, attempted to establish supremacy by adopting a two-fold strategy: by curtailing fundamental rights on the one hand through executive and legislative action, and on the other hand, passing sweeping constitutional amendments in order to ostensibly legitimize their actions.

It is of some significance to note, that in matters relating to constitutional interpretation, the rationale behind two competing propositions of law may be equally cogent. In these types of matters, there are compelling arguments on both sides of the coin. It is in such circumstances that the judge must sit in his discretionary opinion to either accept or refute a proposition. It is indeed no easy task, and the judgment that follows the decision becomes the bed of controversy. Even then, the reason which actually compels the judge to pass judgment may not necessarily find its place in ink. It is the invisible hand of the system that guides the judge, who sits and painstakingly considers the probable consequences and implications of delivering judgment.

A.K. GOPALAN VS STATE OF MADRAS [AIR 1950 SC 27]

Executive action in exercise of a colourable legislation became the centerpiece of the challenge in *A.K. Gopalan vs State of Madras*. Gopalan was a communist political leader espousing the causes of social upliftment for the working class. His passion and activism pierced the hearts of the people. His speeches were evocative and drew out the people's aspiration for change and reform. His leadership was perceived as a threat to the functioning of the State Administration. Gopalan had witnessed India's independence behind bars. He was only released on the demands of the people. Upon his release, he plunged back into the struggle for social reform, and stood in opposition to the Congress government. He was initially prosecuted and convicted for sedition under the Indian Penal Code. However, when his conviction was set aside on appeal, he was once again on the brink of freedom. But then, a Detention Order was passed against him by the Governor, that retained him behind bars.

Mr Gopalan had the uncanny ability to galvanize the masses, even to the extent of inciting the mass public. Although he could be identified as the centerpiece for creating public disorder, the real threat he posed was to his political rivals. Thus, he became a fine example for the executive to test run the limits of the Constitution and witness how the apex judiciary viewed itself in the entire scheme of things in independent

India. Although the constitutional issues in this case were the interpretation of Article 19(1)(a), (d), Article 21 and the amenability of the Preventive Detention Act to judicial review, the real issue was whether the judiciary would kiss the so-called ring of the executive.

The argument principally revolved around equating the interpretation of the 'due process' clause as found in the American Constitution to that of the 'procedure established by law' clause as found under Article 21 of the Indian Constitution. Expansive reading of Article 21 was heavily canvassed, and finally the six-judge constitutional bench was cleaved into a 4:2 majority against an expansive interpretation of Article 21. The majority opinion was delivered by the then Chief Justice H.J. Kania, which was concurred by three other judges who would in time become Chief Justices themselves. Each argument was carefully rejected by the majority, as the Court categorically refused to equate the word 'law' in Article 21 with the principles of natural justice. The majority held that these terms were merely abstract, vague and philosophical. Chief Justice Kania, axed down the fundamental rights and so it came to be that the law in the procedure established is *lex* and not *jus*:

> 'To read the word 'law' as meaning rules of natural justice will land one in difficulties because the rules of natural justice, as regards procedure, are nowhere defined and in my opinion the Constitution cannot be read as laying down a vague standard. This is particularly so when in omitting to adopt 'due process of law' it was considered that the expression 'procedure

> established by law' made the standard specific. It cannot be specific except by reading the expression as meaning procedure prescribed by the legislature. The word 'law' as used in this Part has different shades of meaning but in no other article it appears to bear the indefinite meaning of natural justice. If so, there appears no reason why in this article it should receive this peculiar meaning.'

Justice Fazl Ali's dissent was a historic one. In his dissent, he opined that the term 'personal' did not qualify the term 'liberty'; and 'liberty' incorporated all forms of freedom, including the freedom to move about freely. He was the first to suggest a cohesive interpretation of Articles 19 and 21. He opined that the rights therein are overlapping and not compartmentalized. The right to movement throughout the Indian territory was fundamental to the citizen under Article 19(1)(d).

The purpose of dissent is so that a progressive court of the future may look back and remedy a wrong in the system. In the words of the former Chief Justice of the Supreme Court of USA, Justice Charles Evans Hughes:

> 'A dissent in a court of last resort is an appeal to the brooding spirit of the law, to the intelligence of a future day...'[13]

After about two decades, Justice Ali's dissent became accepted and the majority in *A.K. Gopalan* overruled.

---

[13]Charles Evans Hughes, *The Supreme Court of the United States: Its Foundation, Methods, and Achievements: An Interpretation;* New York, Columbia University Press, 1936. p. 68

As one of the first judgments of constitutional law, the *A.K. Gopalan* ratio set a tone and tenor of restrictive and conservative interpretation, thereby stunting the development of constitutional law for nearly three decades. In the scheme of supremacy, the first battle was won by the executive.

While the individual, although supreme under the Constitution, was restricted and personal liberty was confined on one hand, the Government and Parliament gained strength by asserting supremacy over the Constitution itself.

9

PARLIAMENT'S POWER TO AMEND THE CONSTITUTION

The judgment in *A.K. Gopalan* boosted the confidence of the government, especially in view of the fact that the challenge to the 1st Constitutional Amendment was still pending before the Supreme Court. The Amendment had introduced Article 31B and placed it into the Ninth Schedule. The procedure for amendment prescribed under Article 368 had been duly followed. But the real issue was whether the courts had the power to invalidate constitutional amendments despite due process being followed. This was one of the critical constitutional questions over which the Constitution itself, unsurprisingly, was silent. Although the arguments for invalidating the Amendment were brilliantly ingenious and meticulously canvassed, it did not appeal to the five-judge Constitution Bench in *Sankari Prasad*. The words of Justice Patanjali Sastri became set in stone:

> 'To make a law which contravenes the Constitution constitutionally valid is a matter of constitutional amendment, and as such it falls within the exclusive power of Parliament.'

The momentum of the Nehru government snowballed with its successive victories in 1952, 1957 and 1962 general elections.

In 1952, the Congress Party took command of 364 out of the 489 seats, and effectively had over two-thirds majority in Parliament. With the landmark ratio in *Sankari Prasad* set in their favour, the Constitution (Fourth) Amendment Act, 1955 was passed, which brought 44 statutes within the Ninth Schedule, some of which had no connection with land reform. It marked the beginning of 'Special Acts', which debarred the Courts from reviewing the constitutionality of these legislations. Even this amendment received the stamp of approval by the Supreme Court in *Sajjan Singh vs State of Rajasthan [AIR 1965 SC 845]* and reinforced the findings of *Sankari Prasad:*

> 'In our opinion, the expression "amendment of the Constitution" plainly and unambiguously means amendment of all the provisions of the Constitution. It would, we think, be unreasonable to suggest that what Article 368 provides is only the mechanics of the procedure to be followed in amending the Constitution without indicating which provisions of the Constitution can be amended and which cannot. Such a restrictive construction of the substantive part of Article 368 would be clearly untenable. Besides, the words used in the proviso unambiguously indicate that the substantive part of the article applies to all the provisions of the Constitution. It is on that basic assumption that the proviso prescribes a specific procedure in respect of the amendment of the articles

> mentioned in clauses (*a*) to (*e*) thereof. Therefore, we feel no hesitation in holding that when Article 368 confers on Parliament the right to amend the Constitution the power in question can be exercised over all the provisions of the Constitution. How the power should be exercised, has to be determined by reference to the question as to whether the proposed amendment falls under the substantive part of Article 368, or attracts the provisions of the proviso.
>
> It is true that Article 13(2) refers to any law in general, and literally construed, the word "law" may take in a law made in exercise of the constituent power conferred on Parliament; but having regard to the fact that a specific, unqualified and unambiguous power to amend the Constitution is conferred on Parliament, it would be unreasonable to hold that the word "law" in Article 13(2) takes in Constitution Amendment Acts passed under Article 368.'

Justice J.R. Mudholkar, although not completely dissenting, observed:

> 'It is also a matter for consideration whether making a change in a basic feature of the Constitution can be regarded merely as an amendment or would it be, in effect, rewriting a part of the Constitution; and if the latter, would it be within the purview of Article 368?'

These were the first seeds sowed towards developing the Basic Structure doctrine for our Constitution.

10

LIBERALIZING THE INTERPRETATION OF FUNDAMENTAL RIGHTS

Shifting back to the issues of personal liberty, intrinsic fundamental rights were considered in *M.P. Sharma & Ors. vs Satish Chandra, D.M., Delhi & Ors.*, decided on 15 March 1954 by a constitution bench of eight judges. This was the first reported case that dealt in substance with the right to privacy in India. The case related to the power of search and seizure and the scope of governmental authorities to acquire and obtain private documents. The principal contention was that such exercise of power violates the person's fundamental right guaranteed under Article 19(1)(f)—the right to acquire, hold and dispose of property as well as Article 20(3)—protection against self-incrimination.

The constitutional bench rejected the doctrine of privacy by holding that:

> 'a power of search and seizure is, in any system of jurisprudence, an overriding power of the State for the protection of social security and that power is necessarily regulated by law. When the Constitution makers have thought fit not to subject such regulation to constitutional limitations by recognition of the

> fundamental right to privacy, analogous to the American Fourth Amendment, there is no justification for importing into it, a totally different fundamental right by some process of strained construction.'

The conservative and restrictive approaches towards the fundamental rights were carried forward over the course of the next few decades by the apex court. The social, economic and political conditions over the course of this time had remained more or less the same as it was during the period of the Constituent Assembly, and therefore, the Courts felt that interference with the ratio laid down in *A.K. Gopalan* was not necessary. The restricted views in *Gopalan's* case was followed in *Dr N.B. Khare vs State of Delhi (AIR 1950 SC 211)* to *State of M.P. vs Baldeo Prasad (AIR 1961 SC 293)*, wherein the Court ventured into the internal and external aspects of Article 21. The concept of personal liberty had not been expanded, rather, it continued to be restricted and confined as it was in the case of *Ram Singh vs State of Delhi (AIR 1951 SC 270)*.

KHARAK SINGH VS STATE OF U.P. (AIR 1963 SC 1295)

The shift in the concept and perspective on personal liberty began in *Kharak Singh vs State of U.P.*, wherein the Supreme Court had once again occasion to consider right to privacy. The principal issue of the case was the constitutional validity of the police regulations, which permitted the police to closely monitor potential criminals. However, this unfettered power of the police was grossly misused. The petitioner complained that the police would, inter alia:

(i) enter his house;
(ii) knock and shout at his door;
(iii) wake him up during the night;
(iv) ask him to accompany them to the station; and
(v) ask him to report his departure to the local constable.

The most notorious regulation was No. 236, which permitted the police to make visits to the domicile of the potential criminal at any time in the night.

The constitutional bench of the Supreme Court ultimately held that these regulations were *ultra vires* of the Constitution. However, the majority did not recognize the right to privacy as a fundamental one encapsulated in Part III of the Constitution.

Justice Ayyangar, speaking for the majority, observed that:

> 'The right of privacy is not a guaranteed right under our Constitution and therefore the attempt to ascertain the movements of an individual which is merely a manner in which privacy is invaded is not an infringement of a fundamental right guaranteed by Part III.'

However, Justice Subba Rao's thought was quite progressive and innovative. He was able to holistically examine the situation and scope of the fundamental rights, and more importantly, basic human rights. It was this enlightened thought which led him to observe:

> 'It is true our Constitution does not expressly declare a right to privacy as a fundamental right, but the said right is an essential ingredient of personal liberty... Indeed, nothing is more deleterious to a man's physical

> happiness and health than a calculated interference with his privacy.'

Thus, even in this round, the Supreme Court did not, by majority, recognize the right to privacy as being fundamental. It was interesting though, that both the majority opinion as well as the dissenting opinion cited *Wolf vs Colorado* and *Munn vs Illinois* in their determination of 'liberty' and its nature as a right.

The dissent of Justice Subba Rao later formed part of the majority opinion in *Satwant Singh Sawhney vs APO, New Delhi (AIR 1967 SC 1836).*

GOBIND VS STATE OF MP & ANR. (AIR 1975 SC 1378)

The third occasion where the Supreme Court considered the right to privacy was in *Gobind vs State of MP,* at a time when the Court had gradually begun adopting a more liberal approach to the interpretation of fundamental rights. In this case, the aggrieved petitioner had complained that the constant harassment by the police caused his reputation to 'sink low in the estimation of his neighbours.'

The Madhya Pradesh Police Regulations Nos. 855 and 856 granted wide-ranging surveillance powers to the police. Specifically, they allowed an individual to be placed under surveillance if the police believed he was living a life of crime and empowered the police to undertake domiciliary visits during both night and day at frequent but irregular intervals. The petitioner alleged that false accusations against him had led to the police placing him under surveillance and challenged the constitutional validity of these regulations, contending that they infringed upon his privacy and were therefore violative of Articles 21 and 19(1)(d)—the right to freedom of movement.

The Supreme Court held that the regulations were validly framed in accordance with the relevant legislations and that the provisions regarding domiciliary visits were justified as their purpose was to prevent the commission of offences. It ruled that since only persons who were suspected to be habitual criminals, determined to lead a life of crime, would be subjected to surveillance, the law must be upheld. With regards to the concept of privacy, the Supreme Court was too apprehensive to take 'too broad a definition' as it was a right that is 'not explicit in the Constitution.' It held that the right to privacy must undergo a process of case-by-case development and that, even assuming that the harmonization of different articles of the Constitution led to an inference of a constitutional right to privacy, this right could not be considered absolute and must be subject to restriction to satisfy compelling state interest.

On the point of privacy, Justice Mathew, after intense deliberation, observed that:

> 'Privacy primarily concerns the individual. It therefore relates to and overlaps with the concept of liberty. The most serious advocate of privacy must confess that there are serious problems of defining the essence and scope of the right. Privacy interest in autonomy must also be placed in the context of other rights and values.'

The Supreme Court observed that in case there were any drastic inroads directly into privacy or indirectly into any other fundamental right, the impugned law or regulation would be read down to be compliant with the Constitution, if possible, or otherwise struck down. Nevertheless, after upholding the constitutional validity of the impugned regulations, the Supreme Court advised the Madhya Pradesh government to rely on these powers sparingly and to reform their regulations, noting that they were 'verging perilously near unconstitutionality'.

This judgment evidences the seeds of a slow, steady transformation in the perspective of the Supreme Court regarding dynamic interpretation of the Constitution and respect for individual privacy. The Court largely stuck to a conservative reading of the Constitution, preferring to uphold rights that were explicitly detailed in the text. However, while the Court did not arrive at a determination of a violation of privacy in the current case, it nevertheless acknowledged the possibility of individual privacy being a potential issue that future laws would need to respect, in order to stay on the right side of the Constitution. It is also notable that, despite feeling that its hands were legally tied, the burgeoning pro-privacy activism of the Court could be witnessed in its advice to the state government to consider reforming its laws.

11

FUNDAMENTAL RIGHTS ARE SACROSANCT

I*.C. Golaknath vs State of Punjab 1967 AIR 1643* dealt with both, the restriction of fundamental rights and the extent to which the Constitution could be amended. In this case, the family of Henry and William Golaknath held over 500 acres of farmland in Jalandhar, Punjab. Pursuant to the 1953 Punjab Security and Land Tenures Act, the state government allowed the two brothers to only hold on to 30 acres each, with a few acres being allotted to the tenants on the land and a majority of the land being declared as 'surplus.' The family challenged this decision of the state government in the courts, and the dispute eventually found its way to the Supreme Court via an Article 32 writ petition. In this petition, the family challenged the constitutional validity of the 1953 Act on the grounds that they were denied their constitutional rights to hold property and pursue an occupation, as bestowed by Articles 19(1)(f) and (g) respectively. They also contended that their Article 14 right to equality had been infringed. Additionally, the family challenged the 17th Constitutional Amendment Act, which placed the 1953 Act within the 9th Schedule of the Constitution and thus immunized it from any challenge before the courts, as *ultra vires*.

The Supreme Court, thus, had two crucial constitutional issues to determine, arising from this case: (i) Whether a constitutional amendment is a 'law' as contemplated by Article 13(2) of the Constitution and (ii) Whether fundamental rights can be amended.

The 11-judge bench of the Supreme Court was fragmented along these questions and the final judgment was delivered by a 6:5 majority. The majority of the bench reversed past Supreme Court rulings in *Sajjan Singh vs State of Rajasthan* and *Shankari Prasad vs Union of India.* It was held that a constitutional amendment was indeed a 'law' for the purposes of Article 13(2), and that there was no difference between the Parliament's ordinary legislative power and its inherent constituent power to pass constitutional amendments. It considered Article 368 to be a provision that merely explained the procedure to amend the Constitution, rather than containing the 'power and procedure' to amend. In their view, the power was derived from entry 97 of List I of the VIIth Schedule, which grants all residuary powers to the Union government.

Following on from this conclusion, the majority deduced that since Article 13(2) of the Constitution prohibits Parliament from making any law that abridges fundamental rights, and since a constitutional amendment can be considered a 'law' that comes under the purview of Article 13(2), all constitutional amendments that infringed upon fundamental rights were void. For this purpose, the majority imported the concept of 'prospective overruling' into Indian law, under which future Parliaments would be deprived of the ability to remove or abridge fundamental rights. However, under the purported drive for judicial restraint, the majority upheld the constitutional validity of the 17th Amendment and drew a protective cover over all the laws contained within the Ninth Schedule.

The minority, on the other hand, took a more traditionalist approach, emphasizing that the duty of the courts was to simply declare the law, and such declaration would take effect from the date the law comes into force. They did not believe that the principle of prospective overruling enabled the Court to step beyond this core function.

This judgment reflected an evolution of views and ideologies of the Supreme Court. The majority held that Parliament cannot abridge, amend or touch any of the fundamental rights under the Constitution. But this sudden evolution of views was not accidental, rather it was intertwined with the prevailing political climate. Pandit Nehru passed away during his fourth term as prime minister on 27 May 1964. Lal Bahadur Shastri assumed office thereafter on 9 June 1964. When he entered office, he was already commanding the respect of both, the political fraternity as well as of the judiciary, which was further strengthened by his effective leadership in the Indo-Pakistan War of 1965. However, he also passed away just one day after signing the Tashkent Declaration, on 11 January 1966. Thereafter, a young Indira Gandhi assumed office on 24 January 1966, and unlike her predecessors, she did not command any such deference from the judiciary. This gave the Supreme Court an opportunity to reassert itself as the sole interpreter of the Constitution, which is reflected by the *I.C. Golaknath* judgment.

But unbeknownst to the judiciary, Indira Gandhi was neither passive nor pliable. She was perhaps even more headstrong than her father, Pandit Nehru. Parliament responded to the

Golaknath judgment with the 24th Constitutional Amendment Act in 1971, which expressly provided that Parliament was empowered to amend any part of the Constitution, including all provisions pertaining to fundamental rights. The Supreme Court's ruling in *Golaknath* began a tussle between the Court and Parliament which would reach a crescendo two years later in *Kesavananda Bharati vs State of Kerala*, in which the majority fleshed out the basic structure doctrine to reiterate that Parliament could not amend the Constitution so as to take away fundamental rights, but at the same time also overruled the 'protective cover' that the *Golaknath* majority had created, thereby throwing all constitutional amendments and laws—future or past—open to challenge.

SATWANT SINGH VS APO, NEW DELHI [1967 AIR 1836]

Before, the *Keshavananda Bharati case,* the Supreme Court pronounced a landmark judgment in the case of *Satwant Singh vs APO, New Delhi,* wherein the Court had intricately delineated the balance between individual rights and the state's interests in enforcing the law, in addition to underscoring the need for validly enacted laws delineating executive discretion.

The petitioner in this case, was a businessman engaged in the manufacture, import and export of automobile parts, for the purposes of which it was necessary for him to frequently travel abroad. For this reason, he possessed two passports. Eventually, passport officers in Delhi and Bombay wrote letters to him, ordering him to surrender both of his passports as the central government had decided to revoke his passport facilities. The petitioner thereafter filed a writ petition in the Supreme Court to get the surrender demands cancelled, contending that his fundamental rights under Articles 14 and 21 were being infringed.

The petitioner contended that the right to travel in and out of India is part of the guarantee of personal liberty bestowed by Article 21. Since it was impossible to travel internationally without a passport and since the laws required penalizing anyone who attempted to enter India without a passport, the petitioner contended that the withdrawal of his passport would be tantamount to a deprivation of personal liberty. The petitioner also argued that there was otherwise no law restricting citizens from travelling abroad and therefore the refusal to grant or the impounding of a passport was not in accordance with any 'procedure established by law' within the meaning of Article 21. The petitioner also challenged the unfettered discretion given to government officers to issue or not issue passports on the grounds that it was contrary to Article 14 of the Constitution.

The respondents, on the other hand, stated that the petitioner had contravened the conditions of an import license granted to him, pursuant to which investigations were going on against him. They contended that the passport authorities were satisfied that the petitioner was likely to leave India and not return to face a trial if he was allowed to keep possession of his passports, thus necessitating an impoundment. The respondents also argued that passports were issued to citizens at the pleasure of the president in the exercise of his political function; this made the passport a political document and the refusal to grant access to a passport could thus not be reviewed in a court of law. Consequently, the petitioner had no right to a passport. The Constitution Bench of the Supreme Court was divided along a 3:2 split.

The dissenting minority seems to have adopted an unduly narrow approach to constitutional interpretation, holding that the right to movement was only prescribed by Article 19(1)(d) of the Constitution, which limited the right to the territories of India only. Resultantly, the right to travel abroad could not be read into Article 21. The minority also stuck to a narrow, textualist line of thought, stating that since the Constitution did not expressly provide for a right to a passport, it was inappropriate to 'strain' the Constitution to read such a right into it. The minority preferred to interpret the passport as an entitlement that should ordinarily be granted to an applicant unless there were satisfactory reasons to refuse it to him. At best, an individual would always have a right to invoke the writ of *mandamus* if he felt that he was being treated unfairly, in which case Article 14 would be validly invoked. In the present case, the minority felt that there was a satisfactory reason to confiscate the document because the petitioner was allegedly a member of an organized racket that committed several criminal offences. It also agreed with the respondents' contentions that the passport was a political document.

The majority interpreted Article 21 liberally, ruling that 'personal liberty' mentioned in Article 21 only excludes the ingredients of liberty contained in Article 19 of the Constitution. In other words, whereas Article 19(1)(d) granted the liberty to travel throughout the territories of India, the liberty to travel outside of India would come under the purview of Article 21. The right to travel abroad was indeed guaranteed by Article 21 of the Constitution and thus a passport could not be denied because possession of a passport was a necessary precondition for international travel. A decision of the government to withhold or confiscate a passport would effectively deprive an individual of this fundamental right. Interestingly, the majority view in *Satwant Singh* advanced the minority view in *Kharak Singh*.

The majority also agreed with the petitioner's contention that since no law had been passed by the State to regulate or deprive someone of the right to travel abroad, the confiscation of the passports was not in accordance with the procedure established by law. Furthermore, it was held that granting the executive an unchanneled, arbitrary discretion in the matter of issuing or refusing passports to different persons was contrary to Article 14 of the Constitution.

The Supreme Court had begun taking the liberal and expansive approach in interpreting the fundamental rights, and weaved its authority in the politico-judicial context.

RC COOPER VS UNION OF INDIA [AIR 1970 SC 564]

Popularly known as the Bank Nationalization Case, the judgment in *R.C. Cooper* was delivered in the context of the Indira Gandhi-led government's drive to embrace socialistic economic policies in the late 1960s. The President of India had promulgated an ordinance whereby fourteen private sector banks were nationalized, and thus their ownership was transferred to the government.

This ordinance transferred all rights, interests, assets, powers, authorities and privileges, and properties of the erstwhile private banks to a new, government-owned bank.

Pursuant to this transfer, the central government was supposed to compensate the banks, the total amount of which could be determined by consensus between the government and bank. However, if consensus was not forthcoming, the decision regarding compensation would be left to a Tribunal who would determine the payable amount. However, this amount would be paid out in the form of marketable government securities which would only mature (and thus be encashable) after ten years, and there was no guarantee that the amount would be a full and fair compensation.

In light of this ordinance, the lead petitioner, a director of the Central Bank of India and shareholder of multiple other banks, challenged the constitutionality of the ordinance.

Parliament adopted the ordinance into the Banking Companies (Acquisition and Transfer of Undertakings) Act, 1969 before the matter could be heard in the Supreme Court and the proceedings were consequently adapted to test the validity of the Act.

The constitutionality of the legislation was challenged on several grounds, notable among which was the contention that the Act violated Articles 14 (right to equality), 19(1)(f) (right to property), 19(1)(g) (right to profession and trade), and 31(2) (right to compensation for deprivation of property). As far as the last right is concerned, the petitioner contended that the word 'compensation' contemplates a 'just equivalent' of the property acquired in monetary form, therefore the law that provides for a compulsory acquisition of property must necessarily aim at achieving this just equivalent of compensation. The petitioner argued that the impugned law did not satisfy the test of compensation under Article

31(2) and did not provide relevant principles for determining compensation.

The government attempted to resist these contentions on the grounds that the petitioner's fundamental rights were not infringed as he was merely a director, shareholder, and account holder in the affected banks. The banking companies, being legal persons in their own right, were separate and distinct from their shareholders and were thus not the property of the shareholders. The government also argued that the Courts had no power to determine the adequacy of compensation and that in any case the term 'compensation' did not imply the award of a 'just equivalent'.

The Court sided with the petitioners and held that, irrespective of the banks having a separate legal personhood, the individual rights of shareholders were nonetheless affected and thus the petition was maintainable. Furthermore, the majority of the Court held that although the Act did not violate Article 19(1)(g) of the Constitution, it did violate Article 14 since the banking companies were also prevented from carrying on their non-banking business. Most important, however, was the Supreme Court's evaluation of Article 31(2). The Court held that the constitutional right to compensation implies an equivalent money value of the property compulsorily acquired, and that the government could not award a lesser amount of money. The Court rejected the contention that it was not empowered to determine compensation and held that any law concerning the acquisition or requisition of property for public purposes must satisfy the tests required by Article 19(1)(f). Accordingly, the government's move to nationalize private property without guaranteeing just equivalent compensation was struck down as unconstitutional.

This judgment, delivered by a majority of 10:1, emphasized that the respect for property rights was enshrined in the original constitution and highlighted that the Court would not freely uphold governmental acts simply because they were performed in the purported public interest. However, this judgment was followed by the monumental 25th Constitutional Amendment Act, which sought to overcome the restrictions imposed by this judgment by curtailing the right to property and reserving the power to determine compensation to Parliament and not the courts.

12

THE BASIC STRUCTURE DOCTRINE

The 1960s and early '70s had been quite tumultuous. The Supreme Court had begun developing a more liberalized and expansive interpretation of fundamental rights. Through its judicial dicta, the citizens were enjoying a wider array of rights and governmental oppression was in decline. The powers of government, which had become seemingly infinite were being curtailed by the Supreme Court which declared various actions as *ultra vires* the Constitution.

However, the government was not at all happy with these developments. After the successive defeats in the *Golaknath*; *Satwant Singh*; *R.C. Cooper* and *Privy Purse* cases, the Indira Gandhi-led government had reached its boiling point. The judiciary became an impediment for the government to execute its 'socialistic' vision for the nation, leading Parliament to essentially rewrite the Constitution itself and supersede the judgments passed by the Supreme Court.

Parliament passed the infamous Constitution (24th Amendment) Act, 1971, wherein Article 13(4) was added and Article 368 was amended to expressly provide that Parliament would have power to amend any provision of the Constitution, thereby abrogating the ratio in the *Golaknath Case* and thus, allowing Parliament to dilute the fundamental rights, and further prevent judicial review of the amendments thereto. Even all the surviving members of the Constituent Assembly had openly opposed the 24th Amendment.

After the 24th Amendment, Articles 13 and 368 stood to read as:

> 13. Laws inconsistent with or in derogation of the fundamental rights.
>
> 1. All laws in force in the territory of India immediately before the commencement of this Constitution, in so far as they are inconsistent with the provisions of this Part, shall, to the extent of such inconsistency, be void.
> 2. The State shall not make any law which takes away or abridges the rights conferred by this Part and any law made in contravention of this clause shall, to the extent of the contravention, be void.
> 3. In this article, unless the context otherwise requires—
>   (a) 'law' includes any Ordinance, order, bye-law, rule, regulation, notification, custom or usage having in the territory of India the force of law;
>   (b) 'laws in force' includes laws passed or made by a Legislature or other competent authority in the territory of India before the commencement of this Constitution and not previously repealed, notwithstanding that any such law or any part thereof may not be then in operation either at all or in particular areas.

(4) Nothing in this article shall apply to any amendment of this Constitution made under article 368.

368. Power of Parliament to amend the Constitution and procedure therefor.

1. Notwithstanding anything in this Constitution, Parliament may, in exercise of its constituent power amend by way of addition, variation or repeal any provision of this Constitution in accordance with the procedure laid down in this article.
2. An amendment of this Constitution may be initiated only by the introduction of a Bill for the purpose in either House of Parliament, and when the Bill is passed in each House by a majority of the total membership of that House and by a majority of not less than two-thirds of the members of that House present and voting, it shall be presented to the President who shall give his assent to the Bill and thereupon, the Constitution shall stand amended in accordance with the terms of the Bill:
   Provided that if such amendment seeks to make any change in—
   (a) article 54, article 55, article 73, article 162 or article 241, or
   (b) Chapter IV of Part V, Chapter V of Part VI, or Chapter I of Part XI, or
   (c) any of the Lists in the Seventh Schedule, or
   (d) the representation of States in Parliament, or
   (e) the provisions of this article, the amendment shall also require to be ratified by the Legislatures of

not less than one-half of the States specified in Parts A and B of the First Schedule by resolutions to that effect passed by those Legislatures before the Bill making provision for such amendment is presented to the President for assent.

3. Nothing in article 13 shall apply to any amendment made under this article.

Shortly thereafter, Parliament passed the Constitution (25th Amendment) Act, 1971, to abrogate the decision of the Supreme Court in the *R.C. Cooper* case, wherein it had held that the Constitution guarantees fair and equivalent compensation for the properties compulsorily acquired by the government, and further that such acquisition or requisition must pass the test under Article 19(1)(f)—the right to acquire, hold and dispose of property.

The 24th Amendment had empowered Parliament to amend fundamental rights contained under Part III of the Constitution. In exercise of this self-created power, Parliament passed the 25th Amendment Act, amending Article 31, thereby preventing judicial review over the compensation for the properties compulsorily acquired by the government. Article 31(2B) was inserted to prevent any challenge to acquisition laws on the ground of Article 19(1)(f). Article 31C was also inserted, which provided that any legislation passed in furtherance of the Directive Principles under Article 39 could not be held void for being violative of Articles 14, 19 or 31. Furthermore, such legislation would not be amenable to judicial review in so far as it was a Central Legislation, which thereby stripped the Supreme Court's power to review the quantum of compensation awarded for government acquisitions of private properties.

Despite India attaining her independence from the British Crown, a large part of the nation was still fragmented. In 1947, there were more than 560 princely states spread across the nation. The British Crown had maintained control over the princely states exercising suzerainty, which meant that the princely states had internal autonomy over their territories. Thus, when India became independent, these princely states also became independent from British control. The Indian Independence Act of 1947 allowed the rulers to either accede to India or to Pakistan or to remain independent from both. Ultimately, all princely states entered into Instruments of Accession and integrated into India, and in return, they were granted the privy purse, which, as per Article 291, are regular tax-free payments (royalty) made to them by the central government from the Consolidated Fund of India. These payments constituted a significant outlay from the Central Exchequer and the Indira Gandhi-led government ultimately abolished the privy purse by way of a Presidential Order in 1970, which derecognized the erstwhile rulers and invalidated all their rights and privileges conferred through the Instruments of Accession. The rulers had challenged the Presidential Order before the Supreme Court, in *H.H. Maharajadhiraja Madhav Rao Jiwaji Rao Scindia Bahadur vs Union of India [AIR 1971 SC 530]*, which struck down the presidential orders and restored the rights and privileges of all the rulers of the erstwhile princely states.

Hence, to set aside the *Privy Purse* judgment, Parliament passed the Constitution (26th Amendment) Act, 1971, making the abolition of the privy purse absolute. Articles 291 and 362 were omitted and Article 363A was inserted:

> 363A—Recognition granted to Rulers of Indian States to cease and privy purses to be abolished. Notwithstanding anything in this Constitution or in any law for the time being in force—
>
> (a) The Prince, Chief or other person who, at any time before the commencement of THE CONSTITUTION (Twenty-sixth Amendment) Act, 1971, was recognised by the President as the Ruler of an Indian State or any person who, at any time before such commencement, was recognised by the President as the successor of such Ruler shall, on and from such commencement, cease to be recognised as such Ruler or the successor of such Ruler;
>
> (b) on and from the commencement of the Constitution (Twenty-sixth Amendment) Act, 1971, privy purse is abolished and all rights, liabilities and obligations in respect of privy purse are extinguished and accordingly the Ruler or, as the case may be, the successor of such Ruler, referred to in clause (a) or any other person shall not be paid any sum as privy purse.".

In the Constitution (29th Amendment) Act, 1972, the Parliament inserted the Kerala Land Reforms (Amendment) Act, 1969 and the Kerala Land Reforms (Amendment) Act, 1971 into the IX Schedule.

These Constitutional Amendments became the centrepiece of challenge in the famous *Kesavananda Bharati* case, which is perhaps, the most widely-known judgment of the Supreme Court. It was heard by an unprecedented thirteen-member Constitution Bench.

Swami Kesavananda Bharati was the head priest of the Edneer Mutt, which held large amounts of land in the Edneer village of Kasaragod district in Kerala. The state government, in exercise of the powers conferred under the Kerala Land Reforms Act had imposed restrictions on the management of properties of the Mutt. Challenging the actions of the state government as violative of his fundamental rights, Swami Kesavananda filed a writ petition invoking Article 26—freedom to manage religious affairs.

The 24th, 25th, 26th and 29th Constitutional Amendments were under challenge before the Supreme Court and the issue lay ultimately on whether Parliament had uninhibited power to amend the Constitution or whether there were restrictions imposed on the power to amend.

Eleven separate judgments were passed and a 7:6 majority was formed, leading to the declaration of the Basic Structure Doctrine. What is particularly interesting is that apart from the 26th Amendment—the validity of which was not decided by this judgment, all other Constitutional Amendments were upheld and found *intra vires* the Constitution. The ratio of *Golaknath* was overruled, and the Supreme Court held that Article 13(4) and Article 368(3) were constitutionally valid and thus, Parliament has power to amend the fundamental rights as well. However, the Court restricted the scope of Parliament's power to amend, such that any amendment must conform to the broad contours of the Preamble to the Constitution. Thus, it came to be held that every provision of the Constitution can be amended so long as the basic structure stays the same. Justice H.R. Khanna's judgment, was of extreme significance, as it is believed that this judgment tipped the balance in favour of evolving the Basic Structure Doctrine within our Constitution.

The final Order was passed, which was signed by only 9 out of the 13 judges:

The view by the majority in these writ petitions is as follows:

(S.M. Sikri, C.J. and J.M. Shelat, K.S. Hegde, A.N. Grover, P. Jaganmohan Reddy, D.G. Palekar, H.R. Khanna, A.K. Mukherjea and Y.V. Chandrachud, JJ.)

1. *Golak Nath case* [AIR 1967 SC 1643: (1967) 2 SCR 762: (1967) 2 SCJ 486] is overruled;
2. Article 368 does not enable Parliament to alter the basic structure or framework of the Constitution;
3. The Constitution (24th Amendment) Act, 1971, is valid;
4. Section 2(*a*) and 2(*b*) of the Constitution (25th Amendment) Act, 1971 is valid;
5. The first part of Section 3 of the Constitution (25th Amendment) Act, 1971, is valid. The second part, namely, 'and no law containing a declaration that it is for giving effect to such policy shall be called in question in any court on the ground that it does not give effect to such policy' is invalid;
6. The Constitution (29th Amendment) Act, 1971 is valid.

Interestingly, the judgment in *Kesavananda Bharati* was reviewed in 1975, by the then Chief Justice A.N. Ray, who had formed a bench of thirteen members composed of himself, two judges who had dissented in the main judgment and eight new judges. However, he unilaterally dissolved the bench when he found that no petition for review of the judgment had been filed.

As a fall out of the judgment, Parliament passed the Constitution (42nd Amendment) Act, 1976, which was during the period of internal Emergency. This amendment was almost a 'mini-constitution', by which nearly all parts of the Constitution were amended, including the Preamble. It restricted the powers of the Supreme Court and High Courts, curtailed several democratic rights and gave sweeping powers to the office of the Prime Minister. The Janata Party, after winning the general elections of 1977 sought to restore the Constitution to its former state through the 43rd and 44th Amendments, although with limited success. The Supreme Court in *Minerva Mills Ltd. & Ors. vs Union of India & Ors. (AIR 1980 SC 1789),* finally struck down two provisions of the 42nd Amendment—the provision barring the Court's power to review Amendments and the primacy of directive principles over fundamental rights.

13
RIGHT TO EQUALITY

The actual functioning of the executive is through officers of the civil service—government officers. The premiere officers of the civil services are appointed through the Indian Administrative Services, and with time and promotions may reach the rank of Secretary—the highest position in the Civil Services. They wield a tremendous amount of power and are charged with ensuring the proper administration of the ministry or state government. They are also charged with execution of the policies propounded by the incumbent minister. Therefore, although not a mandate, it was normal practice for the top bureaucrats to maintain political affiliations and allegiances. Transfers and appointments to various posts was a tool used by politicians to place their favourites in certain posts, although neither the Service Rules nor the Constitution permits this.

DEVELOPING SERVICE LAW JURISPRUDENCE AND RESTRICTING POLITICAL INFLUENCE IN ADMINISTRATION

It was in this context that Article 14 came up for interpretation in *E.P. Royappa vs State of Tamil Nadu AIR 1974 SC 555,* wherein the petitioner, a member of the Indian Administrative Service in Tamil Nadu, and being the most eligible candidate, was selected for the post of Chief Secretary. However, he was not appointed to the post. Instead, the State Government repeatedly created new posts and charges with the same rank and emoluments as that of the post of Chief Secretary, to which the petitioner was appointed. The post of Chief Secretary was ultimately filled by an officer junior to the petitioner. The petitioner refused to join these placeholder posts and filed a writ petition in the Supreme Court, claiming violation of Articles 14 and 16 of the Constitution.

The petitioner contended that the transfers were contrary to the relevant Service Rules and, furthermore, the transfers were violative of Articles 14 (right to equality) and 16 (right to equality of opportunity in public employment) because the posts he was transferred to were *de facto* inferior in rank and status to chief secretary. The petitioner further contended that the transfers were made in *mala fide* exercise of power, as they were not enacted on account of the exigencies of administration or public service, but because the Chief Minister (also a respondent in the petition) was annoyed with the petitioner and wanted him out of the way.

Out of the Constitution bench of five judges, three held that while there may have been some plausibility in the contention that the multiple transfers were violative of Articles 14 and 16, they could not ultimately be accepted because there was no adequate material to sustain it. While the petitioner's contentions were premised on the notion that the two other posts were not of the same status and responsibility as the post of Chief Secretary, the majority seems to have taken an equivocating position on the whole question.

Two judges conversely rejected the petitioner's claims outright, holding that the two latter posts were created for cadre officers to discharge high-order duties and responsibilities. They were not created suddenly for any oblique purpose, but instead were no less responsible than the topmost cadre posts. The petitioner was not disadvantaged as far as remuneration was concerned and that both of the posts discharged functions requiring very high-calibre and specialized experience.

Regarding the allegations of *mala fides*, the Court unanimously held that such allegations required proof of a high order of credibility. The bench felt that in cases of public administration, it was necessary for the Court to be slow to accept such contentions on the basis of suspicions and incomplete facts otherwise the effective functioning of democracy would become difficult.

While this judgment resulted in the petitioner's writ being dismissed, it is nonetheless an important landmark due to Justice Bhagwati's observations on arbitrariness being the bane of Article 14, which would continue to be repeated by him in subsequent judgments and which would help form the foundation of the right to equality in modern India:

> 'Equality is a dynamic concept with many aspects and dimensions and it cannot be "cribbed cabined and confined" within traditional and doctrinaire limits. From a positivistic point of view, equality is antithetic to arbitrariness. In fact equality and arbitrariness are sworn enemies; one belongs to the rule of law in a republic while the other, to the whim and caprice

> of an absolute monarch. Where an act is arbitrary it is implicit in it that it is unequal both according to political logic and constitutional law and is therefore violative of Art. 14, and if it affects any matter relating to public employment, it is also violative of Art. 16.'

Indeed, this otherwise unremarkable case produced the judgment that sowed the seeds of rich Indian jurisprudence on the constitutionality of arbitrariness, class legislation, and reasonable classifications. Further, the dynamics of political influence in the civil administration had been brought into public light, which had further upset the Indira Gandhi-led government.

14

VOLATILITY DURING THE INTERNAL EMERGENCY

Since its inauguration, the Supreme Court had been following the customary rule of seniority for appointment of the Chief Justice of India. The senior-most judge of the Supreme Court would be appointed to the office of the Chief Justice. This policy was *sine qua non* for maintaining judicial independence and insulated the judicial institution from executive interference. However, this time-tested custom was torn when the thirteen-member bench of the Supreme Court, by a 7:6 majority in the *Kesavananda Bharati* case, enunciated the basic structure doctrine and curtailed the Parliament's power in amending the Constitution. The country witnessed the backlash of the executive wing of the government, when Justice A.N. Ray was appointed the Chief Justice of India in supersession of three Supreme Court judges holding seniority over him, Justices J.M. Shelat, A.N. Grover and K.S. Hegde. The supersession in the apex judiciary was resorted to by the executive of the day just to assert its supremacy over the other wings of the state. The supersession was perceived to be punitive for the senior judges having delivered judgments against the executive wing of the state. The country as a whole perceived the supersession as a brazen assault by the executive over the judicial organ of the state for having performed its legitimate function, that of interpreting the Constitution. The Executive cherry-picked Justice A.N. Ray over the three senior-most judges in the Supreme Court because his was the lone dissenting voice in the *Bank Nationalization Case* wherein the Supreme Court by a majority of 10:1 struck down the Bank Nationalization Acts incurring the wrath of the then Prime Minister, Mrs Indira Gandhi. In the Rajya Sabha, Mr C.K. Daphtary, former Attorney General for India, then a nominated Member of Parliament, quipped:

'The boy who wrote the best essay got the first prize.'[14]

The first supersession indeed destroyed the finely tuned equilibrium between the different organs of the state under the Constitution and finally it led to the declaration of internal emergency in June, 1975, after the Supreme Court refused to stay the Allahabad High Court's judgment cancelling Mrs Indira Gandhi's candidature in the Rae Bareilly constituency and invalidating her win in the 1971 General Elections, on the grounds of electoral malpractices.

The judicial organ of the state was overawed by the executive's punitive powers in form of supersession and transfer, making the judiciary accountable to the executive for its legitimate judicial functions. In our modern history, the first supersession in the appointment of the Chief Justice of India is regarded as the beginning of a period of aggressive executive control and action which could not be amenable to judicial review.

---

[14]Quoted in: Fali S. Nariman, *'Advocacy in Constitutional Cases'* https://www.scconline.com/blog/post/2016/02/24/advocacy-in-constitutional-cases/ (accessed on 5 July 2019)

With the Emergency, freedoms were curtailed by suspending all the fundamental rights guaranteed under the Constitution. Citizens were left without any judicial remedy in the face of executive onslaught on their right to life and liberty. Lakhs of people who voiced their opposition against the authoritarian rule were incarcerated, tortured and jailed without trial.

After the Supreme Court was subdued and muted as an institution, further onslaughts were mounted on various high courts across the country. The executive resorted to punitive transfers of the high court judges who demonstrated their courage and independence in favour of the citizens. One prime example is that of the detention of the well-known journalist—Kuldip Nayar. The Delhi High Court on a *habeas corpus* petition challenging the detention of Kuldip Nayar passed a detailed judgment quashing the detention order. For this judgment, the Delhi High Court bench consisting of Justices S. Rangarajan and R.N. Aggarwal had to suffer the punitive action dealt by the executive. Justice S. Rangarajan was transferred to the Guwahati High Court and Justice R.N. Aggarwal, who later became the Chief Justice of the Delhi High Court, was demoted to the post of district judge in Delhi. These kinds of actions were representative of the executive arrogance and its desire to instill fear and infringe into the domain of judicial independence.

At the heights of the internal emergency, the second and successive supersession took place when Justice M.H. Beg superseded Justice H.R. Khanna to the office of the Chief Justice of India. Justice H.R. Khanna paid a heavy price for having penned the dissenting judgment in the infamous *ADM*

Jabalpur case, wherein judicial remedies were absolutely denied to the citizens, even in cases where the state action was found to be arbitrary and oppressive.

The overbearing attitude of the executive continued throughout the period of internal emergency and was brought to an end only with the defeat of the emergency regime in March 1977.

However, the slow yet incremental battle towards personal liberty and freedom were all washed away with the onset of the internal emergency. History remembers the judgment in *ADM Jabalpur vs Shivkant Shukla (1976) 2 SCC 521* as the black mark against the Supreme Court.

Eminent jurist H.M. Seervai considered it as the 'most glaring instance in which the Supreme Court suffered most severely from a self-inflicted wound'[15]. Others, including former Supreme Court Justice V.R. Krishna Iyer, refer to this judgment as the 'darkest hour in the history of the Supreme Court'.

---

[15]Quoted in: Ashok H. Desai, *1975–1977 Emergency—Some Legal Recollections* *https:*//www.scconline.com/blog/post/2017/04/06/1975-1977-emergency-some-legal-recollections-from-scc-archives/(accessed on 5 July 2019)

15

POST-EMERGENCY: THE REFORMATIVE YEARS

After the Emergency, the Eighth Law Commission was established in 1977 under the chairmanship of Justice H.R. Khanna. With the experience of the effects of political control over the judiciary, the 79th Law Commission Report was published and it developed the idea that the Chief Justice should consult with the three senior-most colleagues before recommending candidates for appointment. The idea of reforming the appointment process was cemented and strongly recommended in Justice Khanna's eightieth report which was also published in 1979. It recommended setting up a Commission consisting of the Chief Justice of India, the union law minister and three members who have served as the Chief Justice of India or judges of the Supreme Court. This proposal was strongly opposed by the judges of the high courts, and so this also did not materialize.

In 1981, Bar Council of India (BCI) also made a similar proposal of setting up a collegium system. As per the specifics of the proposal, the BCI suggested that the collegium should comprise: the Chief Justice of India, the next four senior-most judges of the Supreme Court and two representatives from the Bar. The Bar Council in this proposal, had also sought to make the recommendation of the collegium binding for the president of India, thereby minimizing the role of the executive in the appointments process. However, this proposal also did not make any headway.

MANEKA GANDHI VS UNION OF INDIA (AIR 1978 SC 597)

As its first step towards atonement for failing to discharge its duties under the Constitution, the Supreme Court enunciated the Golden Triangle of Articles 14, 19 and 21 in the judgment of *Maneka Gandhi vs Union of India*. By this judgment, fundamental rights were no longer interpreted in distinct compartments, but flowed through each other.

In this case, the petitioner, a member of the ruling Gandhi family, was actively opposed to the post-Emergency Janata Party government. In order to restrict her activities, the Passport Control Authority, in 1977, issued a notice for impounding her passport. The petitioner immediately issued a representation seeking specific reasons for the notice of impoundment. The authorities merely stated that the notice was issued in the public interest and did not furnish any additional details. The petitioner challenged the notice in a writ petition before the Supreme Court on the grounds that the notice was violative of Articles 14 (right to equality), 19(1)(a) (freedom of speech and expression), 19(1)(g) (freedom to practise any profession, or to carry on any occupation, trade or business) and 21 (right to life and personal liberty). The petitioner also contended that the said order violated the principles of natural justice, *audi alterem partem*—the right to be heard.

The petitioner contended that Articles 14, 19 and 21 were not mutually exclusive, and rather were to be read harmoniously with each, in order to give effect to the spirit of the Constitution. Weaved within these fundamental rights were the principles of natural justice—including the right to be heard.

The government refuted these contentions and argued that the notion of 'natural justice' was vague and should not be read into the Constitution. They argued that any violation of the fundamental rights must be direct and overt, and expansive liberal interpretations to the fundamental rights should not be given by the Court.

The Supreme Court, rejecting the government's stand, overruled the *Gopalan* case and held that the provisions of Articles 14, 19 and 21 were not mutually exclusive, but rather were intertwined with each other. The Court also confirmed the judgment passed in *Satwant Singh* and held that the right to travel abroad was part of the guarantees contained under Article 21.

With the *Maneka Gandhi* case, the Supreme Court's journey in the quest of its identity under the Constitution was complete. By this judgment, it had gained new-found confidence to do complete justice for all, unencumbered by political influence.

After the turbulent days of internal Emergency, the Supreme Court, thus, restored itself to its former glory and took its dutiful charge as the guardian and interpreter of the Constitution. It restored democratic order and the rights of the citizens through its judicial dicta.

16

JUDICIAL INDEPENDENCE

The appointment of judges to the higher judiciary is a highly sensitive and greatly debated subject. The underlying reason compelling this discourse is quite simple, yet of great magnitude. In reality, the political-judicial engagement takes place in the constitutional courts. The judiciary has been reposed with immense power as well as responsibility in determining the validity, legality and legitimacy of governmental and legislative actions. The executive overwhelming the judiciary with controlling devices would allow for unfettered and self-serving actions and policies, and would reduce courts to being nothing more than a watchdog on a leash. This is precisely why a strong, independent and confident judiciary is important.

Presently, the appointment of judges to the Supreme Court is through the recommendations made by a collegium consisting of the Chief Justice of India and the next four senior-most judges of the Supreme Court. In a similar manner, the appointment of judges to the high courts is by a collegium consisting of three senior-most judges. The appointment process of judges to the high court begins with the recommendation by the collegium consisting of the Chief Justice of the concerned high court along with the next two senior-most judges of that high court.

The Collegium System finds no place in the Constitution, but has been developed by way of judicial interpretation, by the Supreme Court in the landmark judgments of *Supreme Court Advocates on Record Association vs Union of India [(1993) 4 SCC 441]* (the Second Judges Case) and the *President's Special Reference No. 1 of 1998* (the Third Judges Case). The law relating to the appointment of judges in the higher judiciary was developed by the Supreme Court on a reading of the expression 'consultation' occurring in Articles 124 and 217 of the Constitution.

The experience of the British Raj made the Constituent Assembly aware of the inherent limitations of a judiciary subordinate to the executive government. They had come to realize that separation of the judiciary from the executive control was imperative for sustainable growth and stability of the nation. Interestingly, the Assembly also realized they could not radically change the system with the hoisting of a flag. Over time, the British style of governance had become ingrained within the Indian system, and thus the goal of separation of powers, practically, could only be achieved gradually and over generations. And so, the Constitution enshrines the separation of powers under Article 50 as a part of the Directive Principles of the State Policy.

Mr M.C. Setalvad, while delivering the Hamlyn Lectures in 1960 remarked that 'an impartial and independent judiciary was gradually built up in the British times. The Constitution of India continued and strengthened this tradition by incorporating into itself what may be called an integrated judicial system designed to function impartially beyond the range of executive influence and irremovable except by Parliament under circumstances prescribed by the Constitution. A judicial system of this nature was essential in order to preserve and maintain the ideals of democracy and freedom and of the Rule of Law embodied in the Constitution.'[16]

The separation of the judiciary from the executive brings about autonomy, best described by the Latin maxim *imperium in imperio* (a state within a state). The importance of an independent, impartial and unbiased judiciary cannot be stressed enough. The separation of judicial power from the executive and the legislature ideally allows for insulation of the judiciary from unsavoury elements perforating the institution and damaging the administration of justice.

---

[16]M.C. Setalvad, *The Common Law in India*; Hamlyn Lectures 12th series; London: Stevens & Sons Ltd., 1960; p. 200

17
JUDICIAL APPOINTMENTS

Judicial selections and appointments take place within the independent stronghold of the judiciary. As these decisions are not subject to external review, the people of India trust that these decisions are right and further the cause of the Constitution.

Appointment of judges to the Supreme Court and the high courts are made by the president of India under Article 124(2) and Article 217(1) respectively. Article 124(3) prescribes the eligibility of a person to become a judge of the Supreme Court. The 'person' must be a citizen of India and, he/she must have served for at least five years as a judge of high court (or successively served as a judge in two or more high courts), or in lieu thereof, practised as an advocate in a high court (or successively practised as an advocate in two or more high courts), or even in lieu thereof, he/she must be, in the opinion of the president, 'a distinguished jurist'.

Article 124(2) reads that 'Every judge of the Supreme Court shall be appointed by the president by warrant under his hand and seal after consultation with such of the judges of the Supreme Court and high courts in the States as the president may deem necessary for the purpose'.

The Constitution has provided the broad contours for

the process of appointment. Soon after the commencement of the Constitution, the Memorandum of Procedure (MoP) for appointment of judges to the Supreme Court and the high courts were framed. This MoP has been periodically revised—first in 1973 and then in 1983. Two more significant revisions took place in 1994 and 1998 in accordance with the judgments passed in the 'Second' and 'Third Judges' cases. In the judgment passed in *Supreme Court Advocates-on-Record Association vs Union of India (2016) 5 SCC 1* (the NJAC Judgment), the Supreme Court directed for a fresh MoP to be framed. The Supreme Court finalized the revised MoP within seven months from the date of the judgment and forwarded the draft MoP for acceptance by the union government. However, the MoP is still pending finalization at the end of the union government.

In the early years of independence, the concept of separation of powers existed only on paper. The First Law Commission, chaired by Mr M.C. Setalvad, published the 14th Report on reform of Judicial Administration on 16 September 1958, and therein observed that appointments were made on the basis of communal, social, religious and political considerations rather than on the merit and competency of the candidate. The executive had a strong control over the judiciary. However, more than the appointment process and rules themselves, the control of the executive over the judiciary can be attributed to the strong political leadership and the deference of the judiciary prevailing at the time. Over the course of time, as the political leadership weakened, the judiciary became more aware of their powers and responsibilities and had experientially realized the importance of maintaining their independence and insulation from extraneous control.

The 14th Law Commission Report, therefore, recommended for concurrence by the Chief Justice of India before appointing the candidate. However, nothing more became of this recommendation. During this period (from the 1950s to the 1970s), the government enjoyed strong control over the appointment process, though due deference was also shown to the judicial views. Very rarely did any appointment to the higher judiciary take place without the concurrence of the Chief Justice of India. At this time, the appointment process for the higher judiciary ran smoothly only because of the quality of persons occupying the seats of power—that is, both executive as well as judicial.

THE THREE JUDGES CASES

Despite efforts from several quarters calling for reform, the law still permitted executive dominance over judicial appointments. In 1980, the Minister of Law and Justice issued a circular amending the MoP, which was challenged in the Supreme Court, leading to the First Judges Case (*S.P. Gupta vs Union of India [AIR 1982 SC 149]*) which is also known as the Judges' Transfer Case and its judgment was delivered in 1981 by a 4:3 majority. By this judgment, primacy of appointments was given to the executive, and it was held that the recommendations of the Chief Justice of India can be refused by the president for 'cogent reasons'. It was further held by the majority that the Chief Justice was merely a 'consultee' and Article 124 did not envisage 'concurrence' of the Chief Justice of India in the appointment of candidates. This judgment strengthened the teeth of the executive and its role in the appointment process.

This judgment governed the field for 12 long years, deviating away from the constitutional goal of separation of powers.

Despite the judgment in *S.P. Gupta*, the Law Commission was active in recommending reforms. In 1987, when the Law Commission took up the issue again, it proposed an eleven-person committee called the Judicial Service Commission. The constituents were the Chief Justice of India, the predecessor Chief Justice, three senior-most judges of the Supreme Court, the senior-most Chief Justices of high court, the Attorney General of India, the Minister of Law and Justice and an academic in law. The recommendations of this Commission would be binding on the president, although the president could refer the recommendations back to the Commission for review and confirmation.

The process of appointment was sought to be changed in the 67th Constitutional Amendment Bill tabled in 1990. This amendment proposed to change the word 'consultation' with the word 'concurrence' in order to make the consent and affirmation of the Chief Justice of India mandatory. However, this bill also failed in the Parliament, and Article 124 remained unchanged.

With the executive still intertwined in appointments to the judiciary, the public sentiment questioned the quality of the candidates appointed to the judiciary. The system operated in an opaque manner and several appointments were being blocked by the executive in light of the political climate and leadership. This in itself led to a large number of vacancies in the system, contributing to the delay in the delivery of justice.

With legislative mechanisms, proposals and recommendations failing to bring reform in the system, judicial interpretation in the Second and Third Judges cases filled in the vacuum for reforming the appointment process of judges.

With the system ripe for reform, the Supreme Court delivered judgment in the 'Second Judges Case' (*Supreme Court Advocates-on-Record Association vs Union of India*) by a 7:2 majority. The collegium system was established for the first time by the majority in this judgment. This collegium proposed by this judgment, would consist of the Chief Justice of India and the next two senior-most judges. The majority further held that the concurrence of the Chief Justice was mandatory in the appointment of judges. The majority concluded:

> '1. The process of appointment of Judges to the Supreme Court and the High Courts is an integrated "participatory consultative process" for selecting the best and most suitable persons available for appointment; and all the constitutional functionaries must perform this duty collectively with a view primarily to reach an agreed-decision, subserving the constitutional purpose, so that the occasion of primacy does not arise.
>
> 2. Initiation of the proposal for appointment in the case of the Supreme Court must be by the Chief Justice of India, and in the case of a High Court by the Chief Justice of that High Court; and for transfer of Judge/ Chief Justice of a High Court, the proposal had to be initiated by the Chief Justice of India. This is the manner in which proposals for appointments to the Supreme Court and the High Courts as well as for the

transfers of judges/Chief Justices of the High Courts must invariably be made.

3. In the event of conflicting opinions by the constitutional functionaries, the opinion of the judiciary "symbolized by the view of the Chief Justice of India" and formed in the manner indicated, has primacy.
4. No appointment of any judge to the Supreme Court or any High Court can be made, unless it is in conformity with the opinion of the Chief Justice of India.
5. In exceptional cases alone, for stated strong cogent reasons, disclosed to the Chief Justice of India, indicating that the recommended is not suitable for appointment, that appointment recommended by the Chief Justice of India may not be made. However, if the stated reasons are not accepted by the Chief Justice of India and the other Judges of the Supreme Court who have been consulted in the matter, on reiteration of the recommendation by the Chief Justice of India, the appointment should be made as a healthy convention.
6. The opinion of the Chief Justice of India has not mere primacy, but is determinative in the matter of transfers of High Court Judges/Chief Justices.
7. Any transfer made on the recommendation of the Chief Justice of India is not to be deemed to be punitive, and such transfer is not justiciable on any ground.
8. In making all appointments and transfers, the norms indicated must be followed. However, the same do not confer any justiciable right in anyone.
9. Only limited judicial review on the grounds specified

earlier is available in matters of appointments and transfers.

10. The majority opinion in *S.P. Gupta vs Union of India*, insofar as it takes the contrary view relating to primacy of the role of the Chief Justice of India in matters of appointments and transfers, and the justiciability of these matters as well as in relation to Judge strength, does not commend itself to us as being the correct view. The relevant provisions of the Constitution including the constitutional scheme must now be understood and implemented in the manner indicated herein by us.'

The 'Third Judges Case' (Re: Special Reference No. 1 of 1998 under Article 143 of the Constitution) was through a Presidential Reference under Article 143, and the judgment expanded the collegium from two to four senior-most judges. It, to an extent, moderated the powers of the Chief Justice in order to ensure that recommendations for appointment were made in unity and as a body rather than as an individual.

THE NATIONAL JUDICIAL APPOINTMENTS COMMISSION

The collegium system had always been viewed as an interim measure until a fairly and properly constituted commission—a National Judicial Appointments Commission (NJAC), for recommending candidates for appointment was established. This commission has not yet come into existence, primarily due to the difference in views between the judiciary and executive on the composition of the commission.

The NJAC was first tabled in 1998 as the 98th Constitutional Amendment Bill, on similar lines to the 67th Amendment, but this too saw failure in Parliament.

The concept of the NJAC finally saw light in law by the Constitution (Ninety-ninth Amendment) Act, 2014. Article 124 was amended in order to change the procedure of appointments from the veiled collegium system to a transparent one through the NJAC. Along with the Constitution Amendment Act, the NJAC Act, 2014 was passed by Parliament. Although the object of the NJAC Act was to bring about transparency in the system and was modelled to be progressive in outlook, it quickly became apparent that the NJAC was merely a tool for the legislature and the executive to impinge upon judicial independence and to drag the judicial institutions into the politics of the country. Thus, it was struck down by the Constitution Bench of the Supreme Court in *SCAORA vs Union of India (2016) 5 SCC 1*, thereby restoring Article 124 to its original form.

With this, there are now four judgments of the Supreme Court that deal with appointment of judges to the higher judiciary.

18

THE MEMORANDUM OF PROCEDURES

The constitutional provisions for appointment to the judiciary have been elaborated in the Memorandum of Procedure (MoP). It has been in existence even prior to India's independence.

The MoP was developed during the British colonial rule setting out the procedure for appointments to the higher judiciary. The first revision was carried out on 4 November 1947, and the MoP was expanded to include the chief minister of the state and the home minister of the union in the consultation process for appointment of judges to the high courts. This revision met with the resignation of the incumbent Chief Justice of the Madras High Court—Sir Frederick Gentle and the Governor of Madras—Sir Archibald Nye. Both believed that inclusion of the executive would politicize the judiciary.

These events led to reconsideration of the MoP and on 26 March 1948, the Chief Justices' conference was convened. They resolved on the following procedure:

'Every judge of the High Court shall be appointed by the President by a warrant under his hand and seal on the recommendation of the Chief Justice of the High Court after consultation with the Governor of the State and with the concurrence of the Chief Justice of India.'

Dr B.R. Ambedkar had explained the carefully selected wordings of Articles 124 and 217 before the Constituent Assembly as:

'With regard to the question of the concurrence of the Chief Justice, it seems to me that those who advocate that proposition seem to rely implicitly both on the impartiality of the Chief Justice and the soundness of his judgment. I personally feel no doubt that the Chief Justice is a very eminent person. But after all, the Chief Justice is a man with all failings, all the sentiments and the prejudices which we as common people have; and I think, a veto upon the appointment of judges is really to transfer the authority to the Chief Justice which we are not prepared to vest in the president or the government of the day. I therefore think that is also a dangerous proposition.'

Sometime in 1980, the Ministry of Law and Justice modified the MoP, effectively increasing its predominance in the appointment process, and accordingly issued a circular to the high courts and state governments. This became the issue under challenge in the S.P. Gupta Case (the First Judges Case). The seven-judge constitutional bench, by a close 4:3 majority, upheld the circular.

With the judgment in the Second Judges Case (*Supreme Court Advocates-on-Record Association vs Union of India*), the MoP was substantially revised in 1994. The salient features of this MoP, 1999 were sequentially analysed by the Supreme Court in the Fourth Judges Case (*SCAORA vs Union of India (2016) 5 SCC 1*):

'95. Our analysis of the MoP reveals that the same contemplates *inter alia* the following steps for selection of high court Judges:

Step 1: The Chief Justice of the high court concerned has the responsibility of communicating to the chief minister of the state concerned, names of persons to be selected for appointment. Details are furnished to the chief minister in terms of the format appended to the memorandum. Additionally, if the chief minister desires to recommend name(s) of person(s) for such appointment he must forward the same to the Chief Justice for his consideration.

Step 2: Before forwarding his recommendations to the chief minister, the Chief Justice must consult his senior colleagues comprised in the high court collegium regarding the suitability of the names proposed. The entire consultation must be in writing and these opinions must be sent to the chief minister along with the Chief Justice's recommendation.

Step 3: Copies of recommendations made by the Chief Justice of the high court to the chief minister of the state concerned require to be endorsed to the Union Minister for Law and Justice, to the governor of the state concerned and to the Chief Justice of India.

Step 4: Consequent upon the consideration of the names proposed by the Chief Justice, the governor of the state concerned as advised by the chief minister would forward his recommendation along with the entire set of papers to the Union Minister for Law and Justice.

Step 5: The Union Minister for Law and Justice would, at his own, consider the recommendations placed before him in light of the reports as may be available to the government in respect of the names under consideration. The proposed names would be subject to scrutiny at the hands of the Intelligence Bureau through the Union Ministry of Home Affairs. The Intelligence Bureau would opine on the integrity of the individuals under consideration.

Step 6: The entire material as is available with the Union Minister for Law and Justice would then be forwarded to the Chief Justice of India for his advice. The Chief Justice of India would in consultation with his senior colleagues comprised in the Supreme Court Collegium form his opinion with regard to the persons recommended for appointment.

Step 7: Based on the material made available and additionally the views of the judges of the Supreme Court (who were conversant with the affairs of the high court concerned), the Chief Justice of India in consultation with his Collegium of Judges would forward his recommendation to the Union Minister for Law and Justice. The above noted views of the Judges of the Supreme Court conversant with the affairs of the high court were to be obtained in writing and are to be part of the compilation incorporating the recommendation.

Step 8: The Union Minister for Law and Justice would then put up the recommendation made by the Chief Justice of India to the prime minister who would examine the entire matter in consultation with the Union Minister for Law and Justice and advise the president in the matter of the proposed appointments.'

The MoP, with its revisions from time to time, have been an effective bridge between the executive and the judiciary in carrying out the process of the appointments to the higher judiciary.

INSULATION OF THE JUDICIARY

The Constitution has uniquely created a federal political structure that is immersed with unitary features.

The Indian Judiciary not only enjoys political and social insulation, but it is also insulated from vibrant internal and external checks and balances, which are otherwise prevalent in other branches of the sovereign.

As an insulated institution, it is imperative to keep the faith and respect of the people in the democracy. The Supreme Court has been successful thus far in this aspect. It is something of extraordinary remark on how quickly and quietly the internal crisis in the Supreme Court was settled. After the unprecedented press conference held by the four senior-most judges of the Supreme Court, who came out in open criticism against the then Chief Justice Dipak Mishra, the public, for the first time, focussed their attention on the internal functioning of the Supreme Court. However, the public attention on this aspect lasted only a short time; the matters settled down within days and without any sensational event thereafter. However, public attention on the affairs of the Supreme Court lingered on for quite some time.

Justice Mishra as Chief Justice, delivered several landmark constitutional bench judgments, some of which even have propelled this country socially forward, earning India respect from its global counterparts. Thus, despite the internal turbulence, the Supreme Court, as an institution, has earned an even greater amount of respect from the public, and thereby has been able to strengthen its authority and command over the executive and legislature.

The Supreme Court appears to have maintained its integrity and come out of its difficulties. But it is important to understand that this outcome has not been through a happy coincidence. The Supreme Court maintains its supremacy by applying a carefully tuned formula. By judicial interpretation it has given the people several freedoms, creating a perception that the Supreme Court is on the 'side' of the common man. Through the freedom of press and free speech, it has taken a tolerant view on content that would otherwise in tort law be libelous. With a free hand, individuals, corporations, bureaucrats, and legislators are openly criticized. In this frenzy of people criticizing and targeting each other, the Supreme Court has taken a firm stand against the criticism directed towards judiciary and judicial pronouncements, through its use of law of contempt. It has been instilled in the public and the media that they should not disparage the judiciary by attributing motives. The Supreme Court from time to time has set examples, to remind the public to exercise due caution and has illustrated that even sitting judges are not immune to the consequences of disparaging the judiciary. In January 2017, Justice C.S. Karnan, a sitting Calcutta High Court Judge published an open letter to the prime minister accusing twenty Supreme Court and high court judges of corruption. Thereafter, in May 2017 he had passed a judicial order convicting the then Chief Justice, J.S. Khehar and seven other sitting judges of the Supreme Court for offences under the SC/ST Atrocities (Prevention) Act, 1989 and sentenced them to five years of rigorous imprisonment. The Chief Justice of India formed a seven-judge constitution bench taking *suo moto* cognizance in *Re: C.S. Karnan [(2017) 2 SCC 756]*. The bench found him guilty of contempt and sentenced him to six months imprisonment. Not only did this event caution the public, but it also set an example to the higher judiciary to be careful in its conduct. Through this process, the Supreme Court also found a new power in restraining a high court judge from administrative and judicial powers as well as imprisoning this holder of a constitutional office.

The second, and often overlooked aspect, is the application of the Official Secrets Act on the employees' part of the judicial administration. It curtails breach and keeps the bureaucrats of the Supreme Court administration in line. When the orders passed by the Supreme Court in *R Comm vs Ericsson* matter were tampered with by the officers of the Supreme Court Administration, the Chief Justice acted swiftly in plugging the leak and had exercised his powers to summarily dismiss two Supreme Court staff members.

19

JUDICIAL APPOINTMENTS TODAY

Within the span of a decade, from *S.P. Gupta vs Union of India* to *In Re Article 143*, the opinion of the Chief Justice of India with regard to appointments in the higher judiciary shifted from being 'consultative' to 'binding' on the president of India.

But the appointments have had an impact on what the institution has become. Comparatively, there are very few direct appointees, and the judges elevated to the Supreme Court have a relatively short term, having an average of five years till they reach their retirement age of 65. While this creates a continuously changing composition allowing for new thoughts and ideologies, it is also the main cause of the increasing caseload.

Former Chief Justice, Justice Ranjan Gogoi had been open-minded about filling the vacancies in the higher judiciary, an issue which has persisted since independence. Riding along on the back of this Herculean task, the high courts have taken the likewise initiative of the filling of vacancies in the lower judiciary.

However, the manner and criteria on the basis of which appointments are being made leave scope for improvement, particularly on the issue of a mechanism for collating database and laying down appropriate criteria for selection process. Extraneous factors such as inherent bias in favour of candidates having a judicial legacy or elitism should no longer be relevant in the appointment process.

While the combined seniority list of the All-India High Court judges is convenient in ascertaining the comparative experience of the high court judges, it serves little purpose towards the actual decision-making process. The factors involved in recommending a candidate for elevation to the Supreme Court are quite wider than a seniority list and are much more normative in nature.

Paradoxically, while supersession of judges in the Supreme Court, for the position of Chief Justice is detestable, the supersession for high court judges has now become routine. The criteria for which a person is recommended is obscure and the reasons thereof are even more ambiguous.

A wide, normative criteria for selection may not necessarily be harmful to the institution. A judge of the Supreme Court is essentially one of the most powerful persons in the country. The post demands the holder to have a clean character, a vibrant personality, vast knowledge, compassion and good public opinion, amongst a myriad of other factors. It is not a bureaucratic post where seniority and the length of service are the sole factors of consideration.

The judicial system is sustainable only because the people of the country have faith in it and in justice. Therefore, confidentiality is also, perhaps, an integral part of this process, subject to certain riders. While events and activities of the candidate, which would potentially denigrate the post of a judge, should not be publicly aired, there should still be a logical explanation as to why some are elevated over others.

In this cloud of confidentiality, it is difficult not to speculate on the manner and reasons behind certain appointments. While there is no overt political intrusion in this decision-making process, it is hardly a secret that political influence plays a role in this selection process. Generally speaking, the high court judges who are expectedly within the zone of consideration, have built, over the course of time, strong links with their political counterparts. Having an allegiance with the ruling party definitely makes the candidate more attractive for selection.

The internal politics of the judiciary is also remarkable. On 12 January 2018, four of the senior-most judges held an unprecedented press conference in order to apprise the public that all is not well within the Supreme Court. Of these four, three have retired and the fourth presides as the Chief Justice of this country. It appeared to the judges that the pressures of the system had reached its limit and the judges therefore, called upon the public to become more active and aware of the system. Silence leads to a sense of apathy. As the Supreme Court is rarely in the news nor is it in the midst of controversy, the public often forgets to devote enough attention towards the functioning of the system. It had been taken for granted that the Supreme Court was a well-lubricated, organized and upright institution.

The current Chief Justice has been active in recommending candidates for appointment to the High Court and elevation to the Supreme Court. With a heavy backlog of cases coupled with a filing rate faster than a disposal rate, the system is headed towards a collapse. If quick corrective steps are not taken, the judicial system would become unsustainable.

FILING STATISTICS IN THE SUPREME COURT

When Justice Ranjan Gogoi assumed office in October 2018, he took on a board with 55,946 cases pending adjudication. Of these, 35,382 matters were listed under the miscellaneous category, wherein leave had not yet been granted. The remaining 20,564 matters were in the regular hearing category.

After he came on board as the Chief Justice, six appointments were made to the Supreme Court. Now, five months later, the number of pending matters have increased to 57,785, out of which 36,810 matters are categorized as miscellaneous and 20,975 matters are under regular hearing. It may perhaps be too early to measure the disposal rate of matters, but it is indicative that merely increasing the strength of the Court will not single-handedly solve the issues of pendency of cases and the delays in administering justice.

When Justice Dipak Misra assumed office as the Chief Justice on 28 August 2017, he took on a board of 58,272 matters out of which 32,955 matters were under the miscellaneous category and 25,317 matters were under the regular hearing category. This does show that he was able to effectively decrease the pendency of matters. He was also able to deliver a series of landmark constitutional bench judgments which has brought the society forward.

Justice J.S. Khehar took charge on 4 January 2017, of a board with 62,537 matters—with 36,105 miscellaneous matters and 26,432 regular hearing matters. He was also successful in reducing the backlog of cases. His relatively short tenure of nearly eight months witnessed the e-filing initiative, certain landmark constitutional judgments that settled law and affirmed the supremacy of the Supreme Court.

While statistics are not the sole measure of success and failure, they do support certain theories explaining the functioning of the courts. While appointments are imperative, the rapid appointment process decreases the transitioning time of the high court judge to elevate his thoughts to that demanded at the levels of the Supreme Court.

It is interesting to note, that in the midst of all this, there are certain sensational matters that draw more judicial time and attention, at the cost of other pending matters. As each matter is unique, and have their own implications, the Supreme Court assesses the amount of time it needs to devote to each matter. Some matters end in seconds, as they only deserve mere seconds of judicial time. Whilst others draw out for days and months together. The judge has to carefully assess the gravity of each matter and satisfy himself on how much time and attention the matter deserves.

20
PROTECTING PUBLIC INTEREST

Since other branches of the state have been facing a crisis of credibility due to a growing decline in public morality, people have taken recourse to Public Interest Litigation, seeking governance that is honest and free from corruption. Over the years, the focus of PIL cases has shifted from issues of human rights to the issues of public accountability and governance. Through PIL, the courts have unearthed several scams and cases of bribery.

The courts have played a crucial role in unravelling several high-profile scams. One fine example is the Hawala scam also known as the Jain Diaries case. Just before the liberalization of the Indian economy in 1991, several politicians and bureaucrats channeled their bribery receipts through the hawala operations. In exchange, lucrative government contracts and other favours were granted by the politicians.

It was observed in *CBI vs V.C. Shukla (1998) 3 SCC 410,* that detailed accounts of large payments made to people, were recorded in the seized diaries. The transacting parties were only identified by their initials. After carefully analysing these diaries, and through interrogation, it was revealed that these initials corresponded to that of top-level politicians—some of whom were still in power while others were out of it. Transactions conducted by high ranking bureaucrats were also discovered in these diaries.

The discovery of the hawala racket involving the politicians and bureaucrats was purely coincidental. Soon thereafter, the investigation of the CBI abruptly stopped and the investigations relating to the Jain brothers and the diaries were left incomplete. This seemed to be the obvious outcome as the investigating officers of the CBI were transferred, consequent to orders from the politicians in power.

However, investigative journalists pursued this scandal and on 4 October 1993, writ petitions under Article 32 were filed in public interest, with a journalist, Mr Vineet Narain taking the lead on this. In the petition it was alleged that the CBI had:

> 'failed to investigate matters arising out of the seizure of the "Jain diaries";
>
> that the apprehension of terrorists had led to the discovery of financial support to them, by clandestine and illegal means using tainted funds obtained through "hawala" transactions;
>
> that this had also disclosed a nexus between politicians, bureaucrats and criminals, who were recipients of money from unlawful sources, given for unlawful consideration that the CBI and other government agencies had failed to investigate the matter, take it to its logical conclusion and prosecute all persons who were found to have committed an offence;
>
> that this was done with a view to protect the persons involved, who were very influential and powerful;
>
> that the matter disclosed a nexus between crime

> and corruption at high places in public life and it posed a serious threat to the integrity, security and economy of the nation;
>
> that probity in public life, the rule of law and the preservation of democracy required that government agencies are compelled to duly perform their legal obligations and to proceed in accordance with law against every person involved, irrespective of where he was placed in the political hierarchy'

The Jain hawala catered to politicians belonging to different political parties. The transaction amounts allegedly ranged from ₹50,000 to ₹7.5 crore.

Consequent to the PIL filed by Mr Vineet Narain, the investigation was revived by the Supreme Court. The investigating agency also came under the Court's scrutiny and it was observed that it was not insulated from political and executive influence, and thus, could not be called an independent investigating agency. It was in this light that the Supreme Court directed the Central Vigilance Commission (CVC) to exercise a supervisory role over the CBI. This judgment of the Supreme Court (*Vineet Narain vs Union of India (1998) 1 SCC 226*) led to several administrative reforms, including fixing the tenure of the CBI directors at two years, in order to insulate them from administrative control of the political powers.

The mechanism of PIL has largely been a success and has achieved the goals and purpose for which it was developed. Through this, the courts have been able to ensure proper functioning of the constitutional authorities. It has allowed the Court to pass directions on issues ranging from blood-collection and blood-sampling, to sexual harassment in the workplace.

These directions in regulating governance have often been criticized and have been perceived as being against the doctrine of separation of powers. It would appear that the courts are slowly entering into the domain of the executive and the legislature. However, it is important to appreciate that the intervention of the Supreme Court comes at the last stage, that is, when the constitutional authorities abdicate their obligation in performing their duties. The Court takes cognizance of the failures of the institutions and then attempts to rectify or remedy them. That is why, as a matter of practice, the courts first direct or enquire whether due representations, to take action and remedy the situation, have been made to the concerned authority.

The courts are not oblivious to the misuse of PILs. They can immediately identify when petitions are frivolous or filed with oblique motives, and have come down heavily on these litigants.

On 10 December 2007, the Supreme Court came down heavily on judicial activism, warning judges that they must exercise restraint or else politicians may curtail their independence. In *Divisional Manager, Aravali Golf Club and Ors. vs Chander Hass and Ors. (2008) 1 SCC 683*, the bench comprising Justices A.K. Mathur and Markandey Katju had taken a strong exception to the Delhi High Court's intervention in certain matters. It was held that 'Judges must know their limits and must not try to run the government. They must have modesty and humility, and not behave like Emperors.'

The bench thereafter further observed:

'26. Recently, the Courts have apparently, if not clearly, strayed into the executive domain or in matters of policy. For instance, the orders passed by the High Court of Delhi in recent times dealt with subjects ranging from age and other criteria for nursery admissions, unauthorized schools, criteria for free seats in schools, supply of drinking water in schools, number of free beds in hospitals on public land, use and misuse of ambulances, requirements for establishing a world class burns ward in the hospital, the kind of air Delhiites breathe, begging in public, the use of subways, the nature of buses we board, the legality of constructions in Delhi, identifying the buildings to be demolished, the size of speed-breakers on Delhi roads, auto-rickshaw over-charging, growing frequency of road accidents and enhancing of road fines etc. In our opinion these were matters pertaining exclusively to the executive or legislative domain. If there is a law, judges can certainly enforce it, but judges cannot create a law and seek to enforce it.

27. For instance, the Delhi High Court directed that there can be no interview of children for admissions in nursery schools. There is no statute or statutory rule which prohibits such interviews. Hence the Delhi High Court has, by a judicial order, first created a law (which was wholly beyond its jurisdiction) and has then sought to enforce it. This is clearly illegal, for Judges cannot legislate *vide Union of India vs Deoki Nandan*

Agarwal, AIR 1992 SC 96. In *V.K. Reddy vs State of Andhra Pradesh J.T. 2006(2) SC 361* (*vide* para 17) this Court observed, 'the judges should not proclaim that they are playing the role of law maker merely for an exhibition of judicial valour'. Similarly, the Court cannot direct the legislature to make a particular law *vide Suresh Seth vs Commissioner, Indore Municipal Corporation & Ors. AIR 2006 SC 767*, *Bal Ram Bali vs Union of India JT 2007 (10) SC 509*, but this settled principle is also often breached by Courts.'

Thus, the courts have begun to appreciate that they have to remain within their jurisprudential limits.

EXPANSION OF THE CONCEPT OF 'JUSTICIABILITY'

By opening the doors to litigants and addressing a wide array of issues, the public have invoked the PIL jurisdiction against any and every matter which could fall under the brand of 'public interest'. As a consequence, the concept of 'justiciability' and issues which are justiciable have been so broadened that one can invoke writ jurisdiction (which is intended to be used to enforce fundamental rights) to even challenge the constitutional validity of a law for setting up of private universities (as was in the case *Prof. Yashpal vs State of Chhattisgarh – AIR 2005 SC 2026*)

In environmental and developmental matters, the courts are quite often faced with issues of competing interests between individual rights and the right to development. A fine example is the conflict situation arising out of the Sardar

Sarovar Dam. In *Narmada Bachao Andolan vs Union of India (2000) 10 SCC 664*, the court overlooked the impact of the continuous construction of the Sardar Sarovar Project dam on the thousands of tribal people living in the Narmada valley, who, as result of the construction, had been displaced without adequate rehabilitation and resettlement. By this judgment, the Court ruled that the displacement of tribal people and other persons, would not *per se,* amount to a violation of their fundamental or other rights. The Court, on a majority opinion, venerated the virtues of big dam projects for bringing about a green revolution in the country. However, the Supreme Court, later, considered the need for rehabilitation of the people displaced by the raising of the dam *(in AIR 2005 SC 2994).* The Supreme Court ordered that all displaced persons should be rehabilitated and resettled fully, at least six months prior to raising the dam's height.

PUBLIC INTEREST LITIGATION—RECOGNITION OF SOCIAL AND ECONOMIC RIGHTS

The successes in delivering justice by permitting the enforcement of basic human rights on a mass scale allowed for a wider range of issues to be brought before the Court through PILs. After issues such as rights of under-trial prisoners and police brutalities were addressed by the courts, PIL activism was spearheaded on issues relating to social and economic rights.

Sometime in April of 2001, the human rights NGO—People's Union for Civil Liberties (PUCL) filed a writ petition on behalf of the starving people across the country. The Supreme

Court, in its judgment in *PUCL vs Union of India(2004) 12 SCC 104*, expressed its anguish over the deaths caused by starvation. The Court also expressed their deep concern on the failure of the Food Security and Supply Chain mechanism in delivering the rations to the ultimate beneficiary—the starving people. The Supreme Court, through this PIL, laid down that the 'right to food' is a basic human right and thus, a fundamental right, guaranteed under the Constitution. In continuation to this, the Court directed for the implementation of the government's poverty alleviation schemes and also appointed a commission to monitor the compliance of the orders in a time-bound manner. This judgment marked the advancement of society and reinforced the welfare concept under the Constitution. Through the orders and directions of the Supreme Court, the policy decisions of the government have become justiciable and enforceable as a right of the people. Significantly, this decision has also caused a change in the governmental ideologies for policy choice and decision-making.

In several cases, the Supreme Court has taken up the issues of health care and the duty of the state to provide free medical care to the underprivileged people of society. The Court has also articulated the level of care that each person is entitled to. It has held that merely providing emergency medical treatment will not be considered as the state having discharged its duties and liabilities. The right to health is also a fundamental right, and it includes all the essentials required for a person to lead a healthy life. Thus, the duties of the state were expanded to include curative, rehabilitative and preventive treatment.

One of the principal arguments in the government's defence is the lack of resources. The government has insisted that the financial implications resulting from expanding the scope of duties, exceeds the resources available. However, the Supreme Court has consistently rejected this argument and has held that the government cannot escape its duties.

This was aptly brought out in *Paschim Banga Khet Majdoor Samity vs Union of India (1987) 2 SCC 165*, wherein the court held:

> 'In the context of the constitutional obligation to provide free legal aid to a poor accused this court has held that the State cannot avoid its constitutional obligation in that regard on account of financial constraints. The said observation would apply with equal, if not greater, force in the matter of discharge of constitutional obligation of the State to provide medical aid to preserve human life.'

The Court took cognizance of other social goals and objectives of the country through PIL. The courts have played an active role in the progress and development of the Indian society over the past 40 years. In *Unni Krishnan vs State of A.P. (1993) 1 SCC 645*, the Supreme Court declared that access to primary education is an aspect of the fundamental right guaranteed under Article 21—the right to life.

The progressive approach of the Supreme Court has influenced the legislature and the executive in their policies and actions. Originally, the right to education was not specifically enumerated as a fundamental right, and rather, found its place in the Constitution as a part of the Directive Principle of State Policy, under Article 45. Through social activism from various fronts—child rights activists, teachers, social activists, the Parliament has amended the Constitution on 12 December 2002 through the Constitution (Eighty-sixth) Amendment Act, by inserting a distinct fundamental right—Article 21A, which reads that 'the State shall provide free and compulsory education to all children of the age of six to fourteen years in such manner as the State may, by law, determine'. After the amendment, the Right to Education Bill, 2005 was introduced to give effect to the constitutional amendment, and finally came to be passed as the Right to Education Act, 2009 with effect from 1 April 2010. The Act also mandates for private institutions to offer 25 per cent of its seats to the disadvantaged children of the neighbourhood. This process of ensuring education for all, took about 17 years. This reinforces the idea that effective changes cannot be brought about overnight, rather, it takes a considerable amount of time.

The source of the manifold recognition of rights by the Supreme Court has been from the reading of the Constitution. The Supreme Court has also, over time, read the Directive Principles of State policy into the fundamental rights. Article 21, as it stands in the Constitution, is only about protection of 'life' and 'personal liberty'. However, through judicial pronouncements and activism, its interpretation has become so expansive that it now includes a multitude of rights. Thus, the role of the judiciary is to recognize the rights and issue directions for implementation. There may be commissions appointed to monitor compliance, but the underlying fact remains that the ultimate execution is with the executive. The judiciary cannot force the government to open new institutions such as hospitals, housing, schools, etc., but its role in enunciating the principle of continuing mandamus for compliance with regard to the implementation of its directions and governmental policies have yielded positive effects. As a result of this, the legislature and executive have become much more conscious about their role in the advancement of society.

21

SUPREME COURT IN RECENT TIMES

The quality of a society must always be judged by how it treats its marginalized and deprived stakeholders. There are an estimated 60 million to 70 million disabled people in India, but the existing authorities and governance mechanisms have consistently turned a blind eye to their plight. Despite the continuing adoption of laws safeguarding the rights and dignity of disabled people, institutions have, by and large, been negligent regarding their actual implementation. These two judgments were delivered on the same day by Justice A.K. Sikri, a long-time champion of disability rights, and went a long way in ensuring that inclusion and respect for disabled people was not mere lip service contained in the bare acts; but instead is a high-priority goal actively shaping institutional policy.

In *Disability Rights Group*, the Court directed all government-run or government-aided institutions of higher education to comply with the provisions of the Rights of Persons with Disabilities Act, 2016 and reserve not less than 5 per cent of seats for persons with disabilities. While at face value this judgment may seem like a mere restatement of what is contained in the legislation, the threat of judicial sanction was necessary as many concerned institutions were ignoring the relevant provisions and not even reserving a single seat.

The Court also mandated all institutions to submit a list, noting all the disabled students admitted every single year, to the chief commissioner or the state commissioner, also ruling that it would be the duty of said commissioner(s) to check if institutions were complying with their legally-mandated duties regarding reservations.

In the *Rajiv Raturi* judgment, the issue was the lack of accessibility for disabled people in built infrastructure and modes of transportation. The Court noted that certain classes such as blind people or wheelchair-bound people had a difficult time accessing public infrastructure as their needs were not taken into consideration at any stage. Similarly, most information and communication access services were not built with the consideration of accessibility for hearing-impaired people. Despite the government's claims that it was actively pursuing accessibility and making progress, the Court took into account the petitioners' submissions that the government missed several key deadlines and targets and that progress in crucial public facilities such as railway stations, airports and government websites was minimal at best. The Supreme Court resultantly issued a slew of directions to the central and state governments, imposing strict deadlines and ordering scheduled accessibility audits of all government buildings.

The *Arjun Gopal vs Union of India (2017) 16 SCC 310* judgment arose in the backdrop of Delhi's rapidly deteriorating air quality and increasing pollution. A writ petition was filed in the name of three infants by their fathers, who were concerned about the health hazards posed by the increasingly toxic air of the city. Acknowledging that there were several causes contributing to the poor air quality of the National Capital Region (NCR), the petitioners nonetheless contended that pollution in Delhi hit its peak during Diwali time, as the indiscriminate use of firecrackers by celebrants increased the amount of toxic chemicals and harmful particles being inhaled by residents.

The petition focused around curbing practices that particularly affected the air quality, such as seasonal crop burning and the unregulated dumping of dust, debris, and other pollutants. It also notably sought a ban on the use of firecrackers and explosives of any sort during festivals. The petitioners also suggested several policy changes to implement, such as prohibiting the use of firecrackers after hours, restricting the grant of licenses to only low hazard firecrackers, and encouraging the government and public schools to campaign against firework usage. The respondents, on the other hand, argued that there was no evidence to suggest that firecrackers substantially contributed to either noise or air pollution, even during Diwali. They further contended that since the firecracker industry was a massive revenue generator for the state and gainfully employed almost five lakh families, a ban was undesirable and instead a balanced approach was required so as to not hurt the economy and low-income families.

A three-judge bench of the Supreme Court, after going through reports published by several departments and hearing many arguments, issued a series of orders to regulate the sale and use of firecrackers. These orders included, among other things, a blanket ban on the e-commerce sales of firecrackers; a ban on certain types of firecrackers and materials that could be used in production; an emphasis on the point that only reduced emissions firecrackers would be legal; and a prescription for particular timings during designated festivals when the use of firecrackers would be considered legal. Notably, however, the Supreme Court refused to issue a complete ban on the production, sale or use of firecrackers, understanding that manufacturers and sellers of firecrackers still had a fundamental right to livelihood as bestowed by the Constitution.

This judgment is notable because it highlights the delicate tension faced by developing nations around the world—between safeguarding the environment and public health on the one hand and on the other, securing the livelihood of deprived sections of their populace—both of which are essential cornerstones of public justice. The judgment was followed by public backlash and resentment, with certain segments of society claiming that the Supreme Court was trying to ban their cultural and religious practices. However, this case serves as a shining example of the Supreme Court's independence from contemporary political rhetoric, highlighting that it is willing to take tough, unpopular decisions in order to ensure that justice reaches every stakeholder.

SHYAM NARAYAN CHOUKSEY VS UNION OF INDIA & OTHERS (2018) 2 SCC 574

Respect for the national anthem has become an increasingly volatile source of conflict in recent years, and cinema theatres have inadvertently emerged as a heated battleground over the intersection of law and patriotism. While, airing the national anthem, before the screening of a film used to be in vogue during the 1960s and 1970s, the practice fell out of fashion and was only recently revived at a number of cinema theatres, largely influenced by the prevailing political climate. This decision of a number of theatre owners to play the national anthem led to a new topic in public political discourse—the place of the national anthem in the daily lives of citizens. For instance, there was an increase in notable incidents of unprovoked violence and aggression against individuals who failed to stand up while the national anthem played, including in one instance a disabled wheelchair-bound man. Sedition laws were liberally used to arrest those perceived as anti-national for not standing at attention. This conflict ended up finding its way to the Supreme Court.

The Supreme Court's decisions themselves have oscillated between the two sides of the controversy. Despite the lack of any national legislation concerning the playing of the national anthem, the Court in 2016 issued an interim order demanding that the national anthem be played in every movie theatre before the feature film starts. The Court went as far as to prescribe that the national flag must be displayed on the screen while the anthem is played and that everyone must compulsorily stand for the anthem. The Court's motivation for passing these orders was to apparently stress that the national anthem must be respected as it reflects a love for the motherland, and following these prescriptions would instil feelings of nationalism in the populace.

However, the Supreme Court eventually had opportunity to revisit its interim order. After hearing arguments from the petitioners, respondents and *amicus curiae* regarding the limits of free speech, the laws surrounding respect for the national anthem, and more generally submissions concerning the proper occasion for the national anthem, the Supreme Court modified its 2016 order and held that its order regarding the playing of the national anthem in cinema theatres shall be merely directory but not mandatory. The Court was particularly convinced by the Centre's submissions that an inter-ministerial group formed by the government should determine whether or not the national anthem should be played at cinemas.

Regardless of where one falls along the contemporary nationalism debate or the question of whether patriotism should take precedence over individual liberties, this case highlights yet another example of the Supreme Court's concerning trend towards legislative activism. Even while vacating its 2016 order, the Court did not introspect and explain why it felt inspired to issue any directions or rules regarding how private cinema theatres must conduct their business, especially when no question of public safety was at stake. Indeed, even if the motivation behind its 2016 order was to instil feelings of patriotism in the populace, such activities do not fall under the role or functions of a higher judiciary in any civilized nation, and the Court's efforts regrettably could have been better utilized in a more appropriate direction.

ASIAN RESURFACING OF ROAD AGENCY PVT. LTD VS CBI (2018) 16 SCC 299

The Indian judicial system is a sophisticated one, with a comprehensive hierarchy of tribunals and courts, and robust methods for appeal and other forms of recourse. However, while such a structure may be useful in increasing accountability, it is just as much prone to delay and potential abuse by recalcitrant litigants. The core principle being explored under this judgment was the problem of judicial delay; it was observed that many times appellate courts (such as high courts exercising their writ jurisdiction) would issue orders to stay proceedings commenced in lower courts while the appellate court decided a question of law, and these stay orders would remain operational for extremely long periods of time.

In this specific case, the issue that the Supreme Court had to decide pertained to whether the high court could stay criminal trial proceedings on a petition filed by an accused at the stage of framing of charges under the Prevention of Corruption Act, 1988. The Supreme Court held that a petition challenging the framing of charges should be decided within 2–3 months and any stay ordered pursuant to such a challenge must not be unconditional or of an indefinite duration. Furthermore, the Supreme Court used the opportunity to go beyond this specific factual matrix and rule that a right to a speedy trial was a fundamental aspect of the Right to Life and Liberty as enshrined by Article 21 of the Constitution. The Court noted that high courts must not unduly interfere with proceedings in lower courts and any intervention should only be undertaken in the rarest of rare cases. Moreover, the Court laid down extensive guidelines concerning how proceedings in such cases must be carried out in a timely manner. In this judgment, the Supreme Court ordered that all stays—whether in criminal or civil cases—would automatically lapse unless, in exceptional cases, the presiding judge were to pass a speaking order explaining exactly why, continuing the stay was necessary and more important, than proceeding with the trial. However, it was later clarified in 2019 that this ruling does not apply to interim orders passed by the Supreme Court.[17]

[17]I.A. No. 27524 of 2019 in Civil Appeal No. 6088 of 2011

SWAPNIL TRIPATHI VS SUPREME COURT OF INDIA (2018) 10 SCC 639[18]

Transparency is the cornerstone of a free and fair justice system. The citizens of a democratic republic must have accessible information about their public institutions in order to hold said institutions accountable. Indeed, the more influential and eminent an institution is, the greater is the need for there to be public scrutiny of the way it functions. The Supreme Court happens to be one of the foremost eminent institutions in the country, but had unfortunately, for long, resisted making its proceedings truly accessible to the general public. The *Swapnil Tripathi* judgment was a welcome shift in an otherwise unreasonable attitude. In this case, the petitioners sought to allow the live-streaming of proceedings in the Supreme Court so as to provide citizens with valuable information and hold the judiciary accountable to the Constitution. The Court, after hearing from the petitioners and several interventionists, agreed that a public trial is essential for a healthy, objective and fair administration of justice. The Court appreciated that technological solutions may permit it to fulfil its constitutional obligations of transparency more efficiently. However, the Supreme Court resolved to first undertake a 'pilot project' by which only proceedings of constitutional and national importance would be broadcast, and for which prior written permission would be required to be sought from the Court. After the pilot phase ended, live-streaming would be allowed more liberally, subject to carefully

---

[18]Along with Writ Petition (Civil) No. 66 of 2018 and Writ Petition (Civil) No. 861 of 2018 and Writ Petition (Civil) No. 892 of 2018

constructed guidelines. These guidelines would include a bar on live-streaming sensitive proceedings like those pertaining to rape or matrimonial disputes, the adoption of a delay to allow time for screening sensitive information or information otherwise unfit for live-streaming, exclusions on the kinds of information that could be broadcast (such as directions given by the judge to administrative staff), and the provision of broadcast rooms in the premises of the Supreme Court wherein various stakeholders such as journalists, interns, and visitors could view the proceedings.

THE CHIEF JUSTICE OF INDIA AS THE MASTER OF THE ROSTER

The institution was shaken in November of 2017, when rumours of the Hon'ble Chief Justice being part of a medical admission scam started surfacing. The Supreme Court bar was split, some supporting Chief Justice Misra, whilst others were seeking an independent probe and demanding his resignation. Shortly thereafter, on 12 January 2018, four of the senior-most judges came out in an unprecedented press conference and said that things were not in order in the highest court of the country. They criticized the functioning of the then Chief Justice of India, Hon'ble Justice Dipak Misra and the manner in which he was discharging his duties. However, the Chief Justice stood his ground and within a period of eight months, the Supreme Court reiterated on three occasions that the Chief Justice of India is the master of the roster. The first judgment was delivered by a Constitution bench of five-judges *(Campaign for Judicial Accountability and Reforms vs Union of India and Anr,*

[2018] 1 SCC 196), which had taken up the issue regarding the maintainability of an FIR against the Chief Justice as well as the power of other judges to direct the registry to list matters before their own bench. This constitution bench led by the Chief Justice himself was originally meant to be composed of seven judges. However due to the recusal by two Hon'ble judges the strength of the bench was reduced to five. The constitution bench stamped the Chief Justice's preeminence as the master of the roster. The second judgement passed on 11 April 2018, by a bench of three Hon'ble judges, led by the Chief Justice *(Ashok Pande vs Supreme Court of India, (2018) 5 SCC 341)*, reiterated the findings of the earlier judgment. Finally, facing severe criticism the Hon'ble Chief Justice assigned the third and final matter to a two-judge bench presided by Justice A.K. Sikri *(Shanti Bhushan vs Supreme Court of India, [2018] 8 SCC 396)*.

The final matter arose out of a PIL filed by eminent senior advocate and a former law minister, Shri Shanti Bhushan, seeking a check over the powers of the Chief Justice as the master of the roster. It was argued that the Chief Justice is only the first amongst equals and is only equipped with certain administrative powers regarding the composition of benches and allocation of matters. It was further argued that such power is not substantive and that certain sensitive matters require consensus amongst the collegium before being allocated to a particular bench. These administrative powers cannot be unbridled and wielded in a manner so as to prejudice the cause of justice.

The Attorney General, Shri K.K. Venugopal submitted that composing benches and allocating matters require application of mind and it cannot be randomly done. The Chief Justice, when he assumes office, is cloaked with this responsibility and with the experience as the longest-serving judge of the Supreme Court, is best equipped to apply his mind in this regard. When taking office, the Chief Justice also brings with him his own vision for the development of law. The Attorney General also heavily relied on the Supreme Court's own judgment in *State of U.P. vs Neeraj Chaubey, (2010) 10 SCC 320,* wherein the Court had held that:

> '9. .....The Chief Justice enjoys a special status and he alone can assign work to a Judge sitting alone and to the Judges sitting in Division Bench or Full Bench. He has jurisdiction to decide which case will be heard by which Bench. If the Judges were free to choose their jurisdiction or any choice was given to them to do whatever case they may like to hear and decide, the machinery of the Court would collapse and the judicial work of the Court would cease by generation of internal strife on account of hankering for a particular jurisdiction or a particular case..."

Finally, the authority and preeminence of the Chief Justice over the other judges have received judicial *imprimatur.*

DEALING WITH JUDICIAL DISCRETION IN MATTERS OF SENTENCING AND PUNISHMENT: BABASAHEB MARUTI KAMBLE VS STATE OF MAHARASHTRA (2019) 13 SCC 631

The Supreme Court sets the tone for the system of justice administration for the subordinate courts of the country. In criminal justice system, the penal codes specify punishments in a minimum and maximum range. However, the discretion with regard to the award of punishment between the minimum and maximum sentence, lies with the trial court judge. This is perhaps the most difficult aspect for a judge to decide, especially in grave offences. Therefore, in exercising their discretion, judges look to the higher courts for guidance. The offence of murder, under Section 302 of the Indian Penal Code, carries a minimum punishment of life imprisonment and the maximum of death. In this case, the trial court found the petitioner guilty and awarded him with the death penalty, which was confirmed by the high court. The matter came before the Supreme Court by way of a Special Leave Petition, which was dismissed in *limine*, by an Order as *'Delay Condoned. Dismissed'*.

However, the review petition filed against this order was allowed and the matter was taken up for rehearing. The Court, considering the matter as whole, was of the view that the death penalty must be exercised only in rarest of the rare, and ordinarily punishment should be of life imprisonment, as the intention is that of rehabilitation. Thus, while capital punishment serves as a deterrent, it should be balanced with the consideration for rehabilitation of convicts. Capital punishment should not be awarded in a blanket manner. The Supreme Court also observed that petitions challenging the award of death penalty should be heard on merits and be decided by a reasoned order.

This judgment has been heralded by institutions across the world as being progressive, and also for setting the precedent for the Supreme Court to pass detailed judgments involving death penalty.

RITESH SINHA VS STATE OF UTTAR PRADESH & ANR. CRIMINAL APPEAL NO. 2003 OF 2012

The past decade has witnessed the Supreme Court repeatedly adopt a progressive, admirable stance towards privacy. Indeed, judgments of the Supreme Court have been at the forefront of the battle to safeguard people's private information and personal autonomy from institutional infringement, extensive surveillance, and unjust exploitation from both government bodies and private corporations. However, this judgment clarified that there are limits to the Supreme Court's otherwise expansive pro-privacy approach.

A three-judge bench of the Court had to preside over a criminal appeal where one legal question emerged as to whether a judicial order compelling a person to provide his voice samples was a violation of his fundamental rights to privacy as granted under Article 20(3) of the Constitution. Since the issue was not argued before the Supreme Court, the bench refrained from passing any comprehensive determination. However, it observed that 'the fundamental right to privacy cannot be construed as absolute and but must bow down to compelling public interest'. The Court noted that, while the relevant statutes were silent on whether a magistrate could compel an individual to provide voice samples, the magistrate nonetheless had an implied power to do so, granted by the process of judicial interpretation.

While at first glance, the Supreme Court's preference of public interest over the right to privacy may concern several privacy advocates who are used to seeing the phrase 'public interest' used as a tool to indiscriminately chisel away at all manners of rights and liberties, the Court does not seem to have passed an unreasonable judgment considering the facts and circumstances of that specific case. Providing a voice sample does not necessitate giving up any private information or force an accused to incriminate himself, as he is not specifically required to say anything that may be detrimental to himself. Indeed, it is not much different from taking DNA samples or handwriting and signature samples, all of which have, for long, been held as an unobjectionable exercise of judicial power.

FIRST FIR LODGED AGAINST A SITTING HIGH COURT JUDGE IN 28 YEARS

Judges play a crucial role in the maintenance of the rule of law and ensuring that everyone is provided with justice. This responsibility becomes exponentially greater for judges of the higher judiciary, as they must not only ensure the welfare of litigants before them, but are also responsible for overseeing the performance of the subordinate judiciary and laying down the law to be followed in future cases. These responsibilities necessitate that high court and Supreme Court judges be provided with immense power to fulfil their functions efficiently. However, it is just as important to ensure that they do not get corrupted by the power they wield and do not misuse their positions of importance. Unfortunately, despite the universal acknowledgment of the need for judges to be of impeccable character, there have been long-running concerns about the lack of effective mechanisms to actually address and root out judicial impropriety, with several frustrated observers and commentators noting that corrupt or unethical judges can oft-times be virtually untouchable, with national investigating authorities or the judicial fraternity itself being apparently unable or unwilling to actively address the problem.

In fact, the prosecution of judges of the Supreme Court and high courts was not allowed until the landmark 1991 judgment, *K. Veeraswami vs Union of India & Ors.*[19], where the apex court allowed the lodging of an FIR against a sitting high court judge accused of corruption. While *Veeraswami* is rightly considered a landmark judgment which emphasized that the judiciary was not above the law, it is important to note that it did not lead to a radical shift in concerns about judicial corruption. In fact, *Veeraswami* remained the first and only successfully initiated criminal investigation of a sitting judge for 28 years.

This lacuna came to an end in 2019 when Chief Justice of India Ranjan Gogoi allowed the CBI to file an FIR against Justice S.N. Shukla, a sitting judge of the Allahabad High Court, being investigated for allegedly indulging in corruption and favouring a private medical college in a case arising out of an MBBS admission scam. The Chief Justice's decision to sanction the prosecution is a watershed moment for modern times as it reiterates that judges should not allow their power and status to inspire judicial impropriety and criminality. However, it is important to note that one limitation posed by the *Veeraswami* judgment, which continues to this day, is the ruling that investigating authorities must first approach the Chief Justice with relevant evidence and seek his permission before prosecuting a judge of the higher judiciary. This limitation

[19]1991 SCC (3) 655

was ostensibly provided to safeguard the independence of the judiciary, but there have been concerns that it renders equality before the law a toothless concept as the Chief Justice is, ultimately, a member of the same fraternity as another judge of the higher judiciary, thus making complacency, hesitation or collusion a possible risk.

RECOGNIZING THE RIGHT TO DIE WITH DIGNITY—COMMON CAUSE (A REGD. SOCIETY) AND ANR. VS UNION OF INDIA AND ANR. (2018)

Article 21 grants the right to life. But a crucial question is whether the right to life also implies the right to die. Euthanasia is the practice of intentionally terminating a life to relieve a person from his or her pain and suffering. It is more commonly performed in terminally ill medical patients. Euthanasia can be either active or passive. In the former, the death of an individual results from an overt act, such as, being administered with a lethal injection. Conversely, in the latter, death is brought by an act of omission, or by discontinuance of a treatment keeping the patient alive (such as removing the patient from life support). The Supreme Court had in *Aruna Ramchandra Shanbaug vs Union Of India & Ors.* recognized passive euthanasia for patients in a vegetative state. However, one question that remained unanswered was the recognition of living wills—a written document by which a patient can issue instructions in advance, in situations where he loses the ability to give informed consent. In *Common Cause vs Union of India*, the Supreme Court held that the right to die with dignity is a fundamental right and a part of Article 21, and recognized the concept of living wills. The Centre argued that the consent could not be truly informed as the patients at the time of tendering the living will could not possibly be aware of future medical advancements. The Court unanimously held that living wills should be permitted in cases of passive euthanasia, since an individual cannot be allowed to continue suffering in a comatose state against his or her wishes.

22

GENDER JUSTICE & WOMEN EMPOWERMENT IN INDIA

The Constitution is premised on freedom, justice and fraternity which recognizes and guarantees the inherent and basic human rights that broadly include the right to life; liberty; food; shelter; education; and equality in opportunity. Further, equality between the genders is brought about through Articles 14, 15 & 16 of the Constitution. However, religious and social customs had led to oppression in the Indian society, in terms of gender justice. The Constituent Assembly was wary that the society cannot truly be considered developed unless women are afforded equal opportunities and status—they should not be discriminated against based on their gender. To further achieve this equality, the government has, over time, undertaken various efforts—through policy and legislation—to secure women empowerment, with the hopes of ensuring economic, social and political power to women.

Mrs Hansa Mehta had eloquently enunciated before the Constituent Assembly on 19 December 1946, that[20]:

---

[20]CAD, 19.12.1946, https://www.constitutionofindia.net/constitution_assembly_debates/volume/1/1946-12-19

‘It will warm the heart of many a woman to know that free India will mean not only equality of status but equality of opportunity. It is true that a few women in the past and even today enjoy high status and have received the highest honour that any man can receive, like our friend, Mrs Sarojini Naidu. But these women are few and far between. One swallow does not make a summer. These women do not give us a real picture of the position of Indian women in this country.

The average woman in this country has suffered now for centuries from inequalities heaped upon her by laws, customs and practices of people who have fallen from the heights of that civilization of which we are all so proud, and in praise of which Dr Sir S. Radhakrishnan has always spoken. There are thousands of women today who are denied the ordinary human rights. They are put behind the purdah, secluded within the four walls of their homes, unable to move freely. The Indian woman has been reduced to such a state of helplessness that she has become an easy prey of those who wish to exploit the situation. In degrading women, man has degraded himself. In raising her, man will not only raise himself but raise the whole nation. Mahatma Gandhi’s name has been invoked on the floor of this House. It would be ingratitude on my part if I do not acknowledge the great debt of gratitude that Indian women owe to Mahatma Gandhi for all that he has done for them. In spite of all these, we have never asked for privileges. The women’s organization to which I have the honour to belong has never asked for reserved seats, for quotas, or for separate electorates. What we have asked for is social justice, economic justice, and political justice. We have asked for that equality which can alone be the basis of mutual respect and understanding and without which real cooperation is not possible between man and woman. Women form one half of the population of this country and, therefore, men cannot go very far without the cooperation of women. This ancient land cannot attain its rightful place, its honoured place in this world without the cooperation of women. I therefore welcome this Resolution for the great promise which it holds, and I hope that the objectives embodied in the Resolution will not remain on paper but will be translated into reality.'

The makers of the Constitution were well aware of the dire situation of women in society. The nation has come a long way from where it stood at the time of Independence, by and large due to the Supreme Court's influence through judicial dicta. Education has also been key in achieving equality of status and changing societal thought and attitude towards women. Government policies providing for reservation for women have also led towards attaining a balance in power and equality between the genders.

Further, the economic development of a society hinges on maximizing the efficiency of its resources. As women began to more overtly participate and contribute to the Indian economy, society developed and progressed.

Even for a long time after the enactment of the

Constitution, equality of women was only found on paper and not in practice. Although women entered the workplace, they were still discriminated against. The Supreme Court in *Air India vs Nargesh Meerza (AIR 1981 SC 1829)*, interpreted that although Article 14 permits reasonable classification between groups, it does not permit classification on the basis of sex. The issue before the Court was fixation of different retirement ages of male and female staff. Further, female air hostesses were prohibited from bearing children, and compulsorily retired in the event of pregnancy. The Court struck this rule as being violative of Articles 14 and 16, and further stated that such provisions were archaic, cruel and an insult to womanhood.

The concept 'equal pay for equal work' had come up for consideration before the courts as early as the 1960s. However, it was only as late as 1987 that the Supreme Court applied this principle for man and woman. In *Mackinnon Mackenzie & Co. Ltd vs Audrey D'Costa (AIR 1987 SC 1281)*, male stenographers were being paid more than their female counterpart, despite the fact that the work being discharged by them was identical. The Court found that the disparity in pay was only on the grounds of gender, and thus, violative of Article 14.

The right to property for women has been long fought for in the country. In *Madhu Kishwar vs State of Bihar (AIR 1996 SC 1864)*, the provisions of the Chotanagur Tenancy Act of 1908 had been challenged as being violative of Articles 14, 15 and 21 as it denied the right of succession of tenancy lands to the Scheduled Tribe women. The Court found that there was no reasonable nexus for denying the women the rights while granting them to the men.

The courts have upheld the measures for women empowerment through Article 15 of the Constitution. Schemes and provisions for protective and positive discrimination in favour of women have been justified as furthering the constitutional mandate under Article 15, especially in regard to Criminal Laws, Service Jurisprudence and Educational Laws. In *Dattatraya vs State of Bombay (AIR 1952 SC 181)*, the Court held that women educational institutes are permissible under the Constitution.

Protective legislation for women is found, amongst others, in Sections 354 of the IPC (offence of outraging the modesty of women) and Section 125 of the Code of Criminal Procedure (CrPC), which have been upheld as constitutionally valid.

The courts have progressively interpreted Article 15(3) in the widest of sense, in order to ensure women empowerment. Even Article 16 (equality of opportunities for all citizens in matters relating to employment) does not come in the way of Article 15(3). Therefore, reservation in public employment, especially for women, has been held constitutionally valid, subject to it not exceeding 50 per cent, as laid down by the Supreme Court in *Indra Sawhney vs Union of India (AIR 1992 SC 477)*. The Court had, in *Gayatri Devi vs State of Orissa (AIR 2000 SC 1531)*, upheld the 30 per cent reservation quota for women in allotment of licenses for medical stores—which was made in pursuance of the Orissa State Government's self-employment scheme.

Thus, the interpretation developed by the Supreme Court over time is that Article 15(3) does not restrict schemes and policies made for the empowerment of women. Rather, the courts have recognized that women have been economically and socially subdued for centuries, and that there is an imminent need for special provisions so that equality between the genders can be reached at as quickly as possible.

The relationship between Articles 14, 15 and 16 was succinctly articulated by Justice S.R. Das in *Gazula Dasaratha Rama Rao vs State of Andhra Pradesh (AIR 1961 SC 564):*

> 'Article 14 guarantees the general right of equality; Articles 15 and 16 are instances of the same right in favour of citizens in some special circumstances.'

In the landmark judgment of *C.B. Muthamma vs Union of India (AIR 1979 SC 1868),* Rule 8(2) of Indian Foreign Service (Conduct and Discipline) Rules, 1961 was challenged along with Rule 18(4) of the Indian Foreign Service (Recruitment, Cadre, Seniority and Promotion) Rules, 1961. Rule 8(2) mandated that a female officer must obtain permission from the government before solemnizing her marriage. Further, if upon such permission being granted, the government finds that family commitments may affect the discharge of official duties by the female officer, then she shall be compelled to resign. Rule 18(4) runs in a similar archaic line, whereby no married woman shall be entitled to appointment in the Foreign Service. The petitioner further complained that under the guise of these rules, she had been subjected to routine harassment by the authorities, including the chairman of the Union Public Service Commission (UPSC). This harassment began from the time of her initial recruitment and continued all the way to the stage of her promotion as an Ambassador. The Supreme Court struck down these rules, and Justice Krishna Iyer held:

> 'That, our founding faith enshrined in Articles 14 and 16 should have been tragically ignored vis-à-vis half of India's humanity, viz; our women, is a sad reflection on the distance between the Constitution in the book and the law in action.'

In order to ensure participation of women in politics, the Andhra Pradesh State Legislation provided for 30 per cent reservation of seats in local body elections and in educational institutions. This was upheld by the Supreme Court in *Govt. of A.P. vs P.B. Vijaya Kumar (AIR 1995 SC 1648)* and further held that Article 15(3) is an integral part of the Constitution.

As early as 1995, the Supreme Court in *Delhi Domestic Working Women's Forum vs Union of India (1995) 1 SCC 14*, passed directions for protecting victims of sexual assault and violence by providing them with adequate legal representation, assistance in filing complaints and appropriate counselling.

Article 19(1)(g) guarantees the citizens with the right to practise any profession, or to carry on any occupation, trade or business. Mere participation of women in the workplace does not serve to further this right. Sexual harassment in the workplace became a severe threat to the exercise of this fundamental right, and even began to dissuade women from working. It became a veiled form of oppression. In order to curb the menace of sexual harassment in the workplace, the Supreme Court, noticing the lack of adequate legislation in this regard, passed exhaustive directions in *Vishaka vs State of Rajasthan (AIR 1997) SC 3011* to protect women and ensure their dignity in the workplace. Known as the Vishaka Guidelines, they held the field for over fifteen years until Parliament passed the Sexual Harassment of Women at Workplace (Prevention, Prohibition and Redressal) Act, 2013.

There is no straitjacket formula for achieving gender justice within the Indian society. Further, a single-track approach also does not serve the purpose. Momentum in this regard, has picked up in the twenty-first century, and the judicial and governmental mechanisms have been extremely active in striving for gender justice. An in-depth evaluation of the recent landmark judgments passed by the Supreme Court demonstrates the advancements made towards gender justice and more importantly the progression of societal thought and attitude.

23
GENDER AND THE LAW

Gender imbalances manifest themselves in every facet of the cultural fabric, and on some occasions the right to gender equality may find itself at odds with other fundamental rights—especially the freedom of religion guaranteed by Articles 25–28 of the Constitution.

The Supreme Court is often tasked with the unenviable position of finding an acceptable middle ground between these competing rights—a position that it was thrust into, in the *Sabarimala* case.

The Indian Young Lawyers Association filed a PIL challenging the customs of the Sabarimala Temple as discriminatory and violative of the golden triangle of Articles 14, 19 and 21, as well as Articles 15 (prohibiting discrimination by the state on grounds only of caste, religion, sex, race and place of birth) and 25(1) (entitling all people to the right to freely profess, practise and propagate a religion subject to public order, morality, health and other fundamental rights).

The Sabarimala Temple barred the entry of women of menstruating age (between ages 10–50) out of respect for the celibate nature of the deity of the temple, Ayappan. This prohibition was granted legislative backing by Rule 3(b) of the Kerala Hindu Places of Public Worship Act, which allowed

Hindu denominations to exclude women from public places of worship if such exclusion was based on 'custom'. Indeed, the Kerala High Court had, in 1991, upheld the Temple's right to exclude women based on this custom.[21]

A five-judge constitution bench was formed to hear the public interest litigation, which delivered its verdict on 28 September 2018. By a 4:1 majority, the Supreme Court held that Rule 3(b) was unconstitutional, as it violated a woman's right to equality and right to worship. Notably, Justice Chandrachud's concurring opinion went as far as to label the practice a form of untouchability that could not be allowed under the Constitution. It is interesting to note that the sole voice of dissent happened to come from the only female judge on the bench, Justice Indu Malhotra.

Disagreeing with the majority, Justice Malhotra was of the view that courts have to be hesitant to interfere with matters of deep religious faith, no matter how irrational they may seem. She felt that the duty of the courts should be limited to prohibiting pernicious practices such as sati rather than entering into areas of faith. She observed that constitutional morality in a secular polity must allow diverse forms of worship and strive to harmonize fundamental rights as much as permissible.

The Sabarimala verdict proved to be a highly polarizing one. The temple authorities and worshippers heavily protested the judgment, criticizing the Court for meddling with internal religious affairs without cause, with some protesters violently opposing the entry of women of menstruating age who sought

---

[21] *S. Mahendran vs The Secretary, Travancore AIR 1993 Ker 42*

to enforce the law. On the other hand, the Supreme Court also attracted some praise for its proactive approach in securing equality for women in all walks of life, no matter how seemingly unpopular such a ruling would be.

REINTERPRETATION OF SECTION 377 IPC: NAVTEZ SINGH JOHAR AND ORS. VS UNION OF INDIA

Section 377 IPC, for many years, stood as a holdover of the Victorian morality that the British injected into India's criminal laws—one that ironically withstood the test of time and remained in the Indian Penal Code long after the United Kingdom acknowledged the provision as grotesquely oppressive and struck it out of its own laws.

377 of the IPC imposes life imprisonment on anyone who engages in sexual activities 'against the order of nature'. While also invoked in cases of paedophilia and bestiality, Section 377 was infamous for being wielded as a tool to persecute homosexuals.

The legal fight against Section 377 was a long-winded one. The division bench of the Delhi High Court in *Naz Foundation vs Govt. of NCT of Delhi*[22] delivered a praiseworthy verdict in 2009, ruling that the prevailing application of Section 377 was repugnant to the Constitution, and struck it down as unconstitutional to the extent that it criminalized private sexual relations of a consenting nature. The provision was allowed to continue penalizing non-consensual non-vaginal intercourse and intercourse with minors. Unfortunately, this verdict was

---

[22]WP(C) No.7455/2001

overturned four years later by a division bench of the Supreme Court,[23] which delivered an uncharacteristically insensitive and baffling judgment; the Court observed that the LGBT community constituted a 'miniscule fraction' of the country's population and that the Delhi High Court erroneously relied extensively on international judgments '[in] its anxiety to protect the so-called rights of LGBT persons and to declare that Section 377 IPC violates the right to privacy, autonomy and dignity'. The Court held that a judicial pronouncement was not needed on this issue and left the question to be decided by Parliament.

This judgment of the Supreme Court was an undesirable step back from its burgeoning tradition of embracing twenty-first-century ideals and attracted a sharp response not only at home, but also internationally, with even the UN chief Ban Ki-moon voicing his opposition to the Supreme Court's verdict.

The Supreme Court would have the opportunity to right its wrongs five years later, when it agreed to hear the matter again and constituted a five-judge division bench for the same. Fortunately, the Supreme Court distanced itself from its previous erroneous decision and unanimously sided with liberty and personal autonomy. The Court read down Section 377 so that it would only cover acts such as sex with minors or non-consensual sexual activities such as bestiality and rape. Chief Justice Dipak Misra observed, while reading out his judgment, that 'criminalizing carnal intercourse is irrational, arbitrary and manifestly unconstitutional'. Justice Indu Malhotra was empathetic, stating that, 'history owes

---

[23]*Suresh Kumar Koushal vs Naz Foundation Civil Appeal No. 10972 OF 2013*

an apology' to the LGBT community. Justice Chandrachud equated the denial of a right to sexual orientation to a denial of the right to privacy.

This judgment, delivered after a temporary shadow was cast upon the competence of the Supreme Court to safeguard fundamental rights, serves as a shining example of the proactive, progressive attitude that marks modern Supreme Court jurisprudence.

MARITAL RAPE: A CAUTIOUS APPROACH

Whereas the Supreme Court of modern times has otherwise been revolutionary in upholding sexual autonomy and gender rights, its approach to the issue of marital rape has been markedly cautious and restrained.

In *Sakshi vs Union of India AIR 2004 SC 3566*, the Court acknowledged that there were inadequacies in the law relating to rape, including where marital rape was concerned (since Section 375 of the IPC expressly excludes a man's wife from the protection of its ambit). However, the Court left the task of correcting these inadequacies, to the legislature.

This cautious approach was made abundantly clear in *Independent Thought vs Union of India (2017) 10 SCC 800.* This public interest writ petition was born from the aftermath of the Criminal Law (Amendment) Act, 2013, which raised the age of consent from 16 to 18, while leaving an exception under Section 375 of the IPC which allowed a husband to have non-consensual sex with a girl under 18 but above 15 if she was his wife. Furthering the controversy was that this provision was contrary in spirit to the amendment of the POCSO Act in

2012, which also firmly established the age of consent as 18.

The petitioner initiated an Article 32 writ petition against the concerned exception to Section 375, contending that it was unconstitutional, arbitrary and discriminatory against the girl child. In a praiseworthy development, the Division Bench of the Supreme Court held that the relevant exception created an artificial distinction between a married girl child and an unmarried girl child without any reasonable nexus. The exception was thus contrary to both constitutional Article 21 and Article 15(3) (which expressly grants and therefore emphasizes the State's responsibility to make provisions for women and children). The Court observed that the exception violated the bodily integrity and reproductive choice of the girl child and had no measures to address the problem of trafficking. It was held that, since Parliament had opted to raise the age of consent in all other laws, then incorporating an exception that pegged the age of consent for a wife at 15 years was arbitrary, unjust, and violative of the rights of the girl child. The Court instead opted to read the exception down to make it consistent with the Constitution in the following form: 'Sexual intercourse or sexual acts by a man with his own wife, the wife not being [below]18 years, is not rape'

However, it must be noted that the Court was careful to not go beyond the immediate issue involved. The bench merely narrowed down the marital rape exception, but refused to invalidate it entirely. In fact, the Court instead stated explicitly that, 'Parliament has extensively debated the issue of marital rape and considered that it was not an offence of rape. Therefore, it cannot be considered as a criminal offence.' The Supreme Court has stuck to its refusal to act on the marital rape question in the years since. For instance, the Supreme Court refused to entertain a 2019 PIL, seeking the framing of a law to make marital rape a specific ground for divorce. Instead, the Supreme Court washed its hands of the problem by granting the petitioner liberty to approach a higher court with the petition.[24]

DECRIMINALIZING ADULTERY: JOSEPH SHINE VS UNION OF INDIA (2019) 3 SCC 39

The judgment decriminalizing adultery finely illustrates the changing perceptions in our social norms. The constitutional validity of Section 497 of the Indian Penal Code (IPC) had come up for the first time before the Supreme Court in 1954 in the case of *Yusuf Abdul Aziz vs State of Bombay (AIR 1954 SC 321).* This provision was challenged for being violative of Articles 14 and 15(1) of the Constitution. As per Section 497, only man can commit adultery and be punished for the offence, and the woman is exempted even as an abettor. At that point of time, the Court upheld the validity of Section 497, on the ground that the classification was not on gender alone, but was aimed to protect the woman, the family and the matrimonial institution itself, and had then placed reliance on Article 15(3).

As per the scheme of the IPC, Section 497 criminalized adultery by imposing culpability on a man who committed adultery with another man's wife. It was applicable in conjunction with Section 198(2) of the CrPC, which only permitted the husband of the adulterous wife to file a criminal

[24]W.P.(C) No.-000416 / 2019

complaint against his wife's male companion.

In the changing times this provision is viewed as sexist against both genders for several reasons: It criminally penalized men, for up to 12 years imprisonment, for engaging in consensual and voluntary sexual activity with a woman while at the same time, refusing to acknowledge the personal agency of a woman and equating her as the property of her husband.

A writ petition was filed by Joseph Shine in 2017, before the Supreme Court, challenging the constitutional validity of these provisions for both of the above-mentioned reasons as well as on the grounds that no corresponding right to prosecute was bestowed on the wife of an adulterous man; that the sections were blatantly discriminatory against women and that they were repugnant to Articles 14, 15 and 21 of the Constitution.

The government tried to refute the petition by contending that the act of adultery outrages the morality of society and incurs great mental injury on the aggrieved spouse and children; therefore, an outsider who violates and injures these rights must be punished in accordance with criminal law.

Siding with the petitioner, a five-judge bench of the Supreme Court held that Section 497 IPC was prima facie unconstitutional as it did not proceed on gender neutrality and there was otherwise no special reason justifying differential treatment between the sexes. The Court emphasized that the law unduly restricted the autonomy of the individual to make his or her choices with regards to his or her sexuality. Since this may be considered the most intimate choice of life, the Court felt that it should be protected from criminal sanction. The bench observed that the act of adultery did not constitute a public wrong, and that criminal law must conform to constitutional morality. Since the right to live with dignity included the right to not be subjected to punishment except where absolutely necessary, and since the prevailing adultery laws were antithetical to the constitutional guarantees of liberty, dignity and equality, the Court opted to strike down the laws criminalizing adultery entirely, preferring to let it remain a civil wrong. It is particularly important to note here that the Supreme Court refused to make the adultery laws gender neutral, instead highlighting the right to privacy and dignity by refusing to criminalize consensual acts that did not outrightly victimize any innocent individual.

TRIPLE TALAQ: SHAYARA BANO VS UNION OF INDIA AND OTHERS WRIT PETITION (C) NO. 118 OF 2016

A salient feature of traditional Muslim Personal Law is that it allows multiple categories of divorce. Divorce may be effected by a judicial process, by mutual consent, by the act of the wife in limited instances, and, in several cases, by the act of the husband. Within the last category, the concept of 'triple talaq' is quite possibly the most notorious mode of divorce. Triple talaq allows a husband to legally divorce his wife simply by pronouncing *talaq* (the Arabic word for 'divorce') three times. This pronouncement may be either verbal or written and is understood to be effective immediately upon completion of the third *talaq* and is irrevocable. The status of triple talaq is controversial even within Islamic Law, with certain schools of thought prohibiting the practice and even certain Islamic Republics such as Pakistan, Afghanistan and Saudi Arabia banning it. In India, the practice has attracted immense opposition from Muslim women, liberal Muslims, and Hindu nationalists. On the other hand, the All India Muslim Personal Law Board is in favour of retaining the legal status of the practice, maintaining that the State has no right to intervene in religious matters.

A five-judge bench of the Supreme Court consolidated several petitions in *Shayara Bano* to determine the validity of triple talaq as well as its character as an essential religious practice. By a 3:2 majority, the Court eventually held that triple talaq was unconstitutional.

The majority judgment of Justices Kurian Joseph and U.U. Lalit and the concurring opinion of Justice Nariman held that, as per Article 25 of the Constitution, the state can only infringe upon religious practices if they are arbitrary and not essential practices. Tracing the trajectory of Islamic law, the Justices held that triple talaq cannot be considered an essential aspect of Islamic law and that merely existing for a long period of time or being practised by several people is not enough to qualify it as such. Justice Nariman also emphasized the irrevocable nature of triple talaq, observing that it did not leave any scope for reconciliation.

On the other hand, the minority comprising of Chief Justice Kehar and Justice Nazeer held that triple talaq was indeed an essential part of the Islamic religion. Acknowledging that the practice may be considered as gender-discriminatory, this could be addressed by legislation rather than a judicial pronouncement.

While the triple talaq judgment may, in a sense, be considered a revolutionary judgment for safeguarding the rights of Muslim women in India, it must be noted here that the Supreme Court seems to have taken the easy way out. The bench mainly considered whether or not triple talaq was an essential part of Islam instead of keeping the focus on women empowerment. It appears that the Court was more deferential to a religious ideology than the autonomy and dignity of citizens, in stark contrast to its other recent verdicts. It would perhaps have been preferable if the Court had firmly acknowledged that Article 25 of the Constitution expressly provided that any practice that is inconsistent with fundamental rights is liable to be struck down, irrespective of, whether or not, it is an essential religious practice and proceeded from that logical starting point.

The Supreme Court has periodically passed judgments to ensure the upliftment and protection of women. Gender justice, in a historical sense, is not only equal opportunity for all members of the society, but also includes protection, relief and mitigation against threats that women are particularly susceptible to. Although substantial progress has been made, a substantial distance is yet to be covered by the nation to reach the point of substantive gender justice.

24
THE EMERGING ISSUES

PRIVACY AND DATA PROTECTION

Unlike the Constitutions of jurisdictions such as Germany[25] or the USA[26], the Constitution of India does not expressly guarantee the right to privacy for its citizens. In fact, this lacuna was acknowledged in 1954 by an eight-judge bench of the Supreme Court of India in *M.P. Sharma vs Satish Chandra*, where it was observed that:[27]

> A power of search and seizure is, in any system of jurisprudence, an overriding power of the State for the protection of social security and that power is necessarily regulated by law. When the Constitution makers have thought fit not to subject such regulation to constitutional limitations by recognition of the fundamental right to privacy, analogous to the American Fourth Amendment, there is no justification for importing into it, a totally different fundamental right by some process of strained construction.

---

[25]Constitution of Germany Art. 2 para. 1, and Art. 1 para. 1
[26]USA Constitution, 4th Amendment
[27]1954 AIR 300

This rigid reading of the Constitution stayed strong, even nine years later in *Kharak Singh vs State of U.P.*[28] where a six-judge bench of the court observed that there was no fundamental right to privacy and therefore an alleged dacoit, could not use that principle, as a shield against intrusive state surveillance and monitoring. However, a glimmer of hope emerged in Justices Shah and Subba Rao's dissenting opinion, where they acknowledged that, 'nothing is more deleterious to a man's physical happiness and health than a calculated interference with his privacy'. Their proposed solution was to interpret Article 21, which guarantees every person the right to life and liberty, to include the right to privacy. Their proposal was finally adopted in 1975 by a three-judge bench in *Govind Singh vs State of MP*[29], which formally acknowledged that the right to privacy was subsumed under Article 21. However, they observed that this right was not absolute and could be deprived by the procedure established by law.

The years following economic liberalization witnessed a bolder acknowledgement of privacy as a right. For instance, in *R. Rajagopal vs State of Tamil Nadu*[30] the Supreme Court had to address the tension between the freedom of the press and the right to privacy. Justice B.P. Jeevan Reddy acknowledged that the latter had acquired a constitutional status and held that the press was free to publish a biography on an individual without his authorization or consent only as long as they relied on public records to do so and did not breach his privacy. The Supreme Court's 1996 judgment in *PUCL vs Union of*

---

[28]1963 AIR 1295
[29]1975 AIR 1378
[30]1995 AIR 264

India[31] further drove home this point, but this time with a message for the government rather than private media. The bench of Justices K. Singh and S.S. Ahmed, frowned upon the widespread, unchecked use of phone tapping and electronic surveillance by the government. The bench formulated certain procedural safeguards to ensure that the government could not indiscriminately use the excuse of 'security' to violate the populace's right to privacy. In *Selvi vs State of Karnataka*[32] the Supreme Court emphasized that in addition to 'physical privacy', there also exists a concept of 'mental privacy'. It was held that the use of enhanced interrogation techniques such as polygraph tests and brain resonance imaging were a violation of an individual's right to privacy.

The Supreme Court has indeed come a long way from its inflexible reading of the constitution six decades ago, and it is now pretty much taken for granted that, despite what the literal text says, the right to privacy is indeed enshrined in the Indian Constitution. This was reiterated in the most important Indian privacy case of modern times, *Justice Puttaswamy (Retd) and Anr. vs Union of India and Ors.*[33] A nine-judge bench unanimously held that, 'the right to privacy is protected as an intrinsic part of the right to life and personal liberty under Article 21 and as a part of the freedoms guaranteed by Part III of the Constitution'. The *Kharak Singh* and *MP Sharma* judgements, which for long had been relied on by the government as a crutch to justify privacy breaches, were explicitly overruled and relegated to the jurisprudential

[31]AIR 1997 SC 568

[32]Criminal Appeal No. 1267 of 2004

[33]W.P. (Civil) No 494 of 2012

grave. This judgment on privacy laid the foundation for subsequent progressive judicial pronouncements, such as the decriminalization of adultery[34] and consensual homosexual relations.[35]

Despite the Supreme Court's proactive role in affirming the importance of individual privacy in collective welfare, there are several emerging challenges which will continue to toss up complicated questions of law and policy for the years to come. The prime source of these emerging challenges also happens to be the primary driver of human advancement—technological innovation.

TECHNOLOGICAL CHALLENGES AND PRIVACY LAW

According to 'Moore's Law', technological growth advances along an exponential curve. What this implies is that every few years, the technological framework shifts so rapidly that the existing regulatory and legislative framework is ill-equipped to tackle it. The law is generally too slow to catch up with technology. This may throw up several undesirable situations. Sometimes legacy regulations are slow to take stock of new technology and impose dated procedural requirements. For instance, the Internet infrastructure and digital payments networks have existed for several years, yet e-stamping of documents is still not possible in most states. In other cases, the legal vacuum may allow widespread abuse of technology before regulators and legislators wisen up to address loopholes. For example, despite the government unveiling the Unified-

[34]*Joseph Shine vs Union of India W.P. (Crl.) No. 194 of 2017*
[35]*Navtej Singh Johar vs Union of India W. P. (Crl.) No. 76 of 2016*

Payments-Interface (UPI) in 2016, it took until 2018 for the RBI to formulate guidelines to affix liability in cases of digital payments fraud.[36] In certain cases, technological paranoia and vested interests may inspire the government to institute knee-jerk bans, thus making society lose out on the benefits of the technology.

With the current digital framework shifting into Web 3.0, where multiple devices and softwares are repeatedly communicating with each other and access to information technology resources is becoming steadily democratized, the one area of law that requires the most skillful evolution is privacy law.

Along with the legislature, the judiciary will remain an important vehicle to steer the progress of privacy law as the country continues to be inundated with new processes and technologies. However, the war for privacy will be waged on two fronts: One against the state and one against private corporations.

PRIVACY LAW AND THE PRIVATE SECTOR

Technology, over the last two decades has advanced at an unprecedented level. Almost all parts of our lives are connected with some form of smart technology. There has been a race by companies, as well as government institutions, to gather maximum data over individuals—from our biometrics to our social preferences. The idea is to create a predictive model for individual human behaviour and to also closely monitor certain

---

[36]https://rbidocs.rbi.org.in/rdocs/AnnualReport/PDFs/0ANREPORT201718077745EC9A874DB38C991F580ED14242.PDFpg 119

types and groups of people. With a data-bank of all individuals, governmental and private control becomes much easier. This also serves in handling potential threats to an administration, as the government can easily obtain confidential data from private entities. While data-aggregation would have some merit in dealing with issues of terrorism and state security, such authority to obtain data tends to be misused against genuine dissenters. This is a big challenge in preserving basic human rights of freedom of speech, and expression.

The common man, apart from being mildly disgruntled, would not care enough to stop or limit his use of technology and data-collecting sites, especially since it doesn't cost him any money. Neither would he take any active measures in protecting his virtual identity. People only see the part of the iceberg that is floating above the water, and so, are willing to sacrifice their privacy and give up their personal data for convenience. However, we stand on a very slippery slope because there is an immeasurable potential for abuse of our data, be it by the government, political bodies, by private entities or even by fringe and criminal outfits. Further, private entities are also being contracted by the government to carry out data collection and surveillance over their citizens.

China serves as a fine example where its political agenda is being carried out with the aid of data collection in the form of video surveillance, face-recognition technology, social media monitoring and telephone monitoring. The Uighur ethnic minority have been actively targeted through China's artificial intelligence software and are being systematically detained in concentration camps.

The dependency over technology may have crossed the

point beyond correction. Therefore, the alternative is to develop a strong regulatory framework to prevent abuse by any authority, institution, or entity.

The Indian legal framework has steadily begun to respond to such risks in light of global controversies and Parliament has unveiled its own Draft Data Protection Bill. The Bill lays down norms for the collection and processing of data. Some key highlights include:

- Setting the conditions for when data may be processed (namely, with consent of the subject, when there is a medical emergency, or for the government to provide benefits).
- An acknowledgement that the subject of the data (or the 'data principal') is the ultimate owner of the information, and thus has rights to correct or seek access to their data.
- A requirement for data collecting and processing organizations (data fiduciaries) to notify individuals of the nature and purpose of data processing.
- Data localization norms to ensure that critical pieces of information are stored solely within the country and not transmitted beyond national borders.
- The institution of a national Data Protection Authority (DPA) to monitor the activities of data fiduciaries.

It must be noted that the Bill still allows certain exemptions from data protection norms for limited purposes, such as national security, investigation of offences, journalism, and legal proceedings.

The move towards mandatory data localization is a policy shift being evidenced throughout a variety of laws and regulations. Examples include, the RBI instituting data localization regulations for fintech companies, third party vendors and payment services providers,[37] the Draft National E-Commerce Policy,[38] and amendments to the Drugs and Cosmetics Rules, 1945.[39]

However, considering the nature of communication over wireless networks, it is likely that the intervention of the judiciary will be called in sooner than later. The breach of data localization norms is a crisis that requires an immediate response and it is imperative that the Indian higher judiciary is well-informed about the nature of data processing and management so that it can lay down adequate jurisprudential norms for the rest of the courts to follow when the time comes. It may, perhaps, be of some value for the Data Protection Authority to refer urgent questions of privacy law directly to the Supreme Court or concerned high courts for speedy redressal, so that delay and risk is minimized.

Regardless of what data protection framework is developed, the complexity of social interactions and the needs for economic efficiency, will require that the law impose minimal obstacles in the freedom of corporations to conduct business. There will still remain quite a bit of flexibility for corporations to set the terms of information engagement and utilization vis-à-vis their users.

A major factor that allows technology corporations to collect and process user data is the esoteric, long-winded

---

[37]https://www.rbi.org.in/scripts/NotificationUser.aspx?Id=11244

[38]https://dipp.gov.in/sites/default/files/DraftNational_e-commerce_Policy_23February2019.pdf

[39]https://www.medianama.com/wp-content/uploads/1890431.pdf

nature of user terms and conditions. It is a known fact that hardly anyone reads the terms and conditions of the apps and software they use. In fact, a Norwegian consumer agency undertook a smartphone terms of service 'readathon' to underscore the ridiculous length of digital contracts contained in the average smartphone—an endeavour that took up almost 32 hours (not including time taken to actually understand what was written).[40]

Regardless of what consumer and data protection laws are developed, the integrity of contract law will require that individuals are held to their end of the bargain regardless of whether they clicked 'I Accept' without even a cursory glance at the text. However, perhaps, there could be a middle ground, devised to address the needs of all stakeholders involved. It might be useful, for user terms and conditions, to specifically highlight and emphasize specific clauses that may pose a unique burden on user privacy. The norms for acceptable terms could be developed by a representative committee made up of consumer protection bodies and representatives of technology companies, and adhering to these norms of contract writing would be compulsory for all corporations working in the information technology space. The Supreme Court would play a much-needed role in giving judicial backing to these norms, which would be well in line with Lord Denning's famous 'red-hand rule', where he observed that, 'Some [unfair] clauses... would need to be printed in red ink on the face of the document with a red hand pointing to it before the notice could be held to be sufficient.'[41]

---

[40]https://www.bbc.com/news/world-europe-36378215
[41]*J Spurling Ltd vs Bradshaw [1956] EWCA Civ 3*

While most progressive Supreme Court jurisprudence relating to privacy law has developed with a focus on protecting citizens from unreasonable violations from the government, there is still much left to be desired.

The Supreme Court returned a widely-reported and polarizing verdict where the majority held that Aadhaar, a centralized database of demographic and biometric information, was not violative of the right to privacy. Justice Chandrachud, in his dissenting opinion, delivered a scathing attack upon the entire scheme, terming it unconstitutional and exceeding the permissible limits for invasion of privacy. Even the majority bench was careful to acknowledge the importance of tempering the system's ability to compromise the privacy of citizens, and prohibited several clauses of the Aadhaar Act, such as ordering that the government could not refuse to render essential services to citizens without an Aadhaar card, prohibiting private entities from utilizing the ecosystem, and mandating that any person whose personal information is at risk of being released by court order be first given a hearing and a right to challenge the order.[42]

Keeping aside the discussion of whether a national biometric database of citizens truly is violative of the right to privacy, one thing that is clear is that the government has not done its best to safeguard the large demographic database at its disposal. Several Aadhaar details given to government agencies are unsecured and can appear in a simple Google

[42]*K.S. Puttaswamy vs Union of India (Aadhaar-5 Judge), (2019) 1 SCC 1*

search.[43] Illegal services sell UIDAI database access for 500 rupees.[44] While undoubtedly the primary liability remains with the government for failing to ensure the security of sensitive personal information, the Supreme Court must also take proactive cognizance of these ongoing problems and take responsibility in minimizing misuse of an ecosystem that it had a role in green lighting. The Supreme Court has thus far taken a passive role in the privacy controversy, addressing issues as and when they arise and travel up the judicial ladder. Perhaps it is now time for it to be forward-looking and ensure that privacy controversies are dealt with before they even arise.

Despite repeated court judgments tempering executive overreach, the rise of new technologies is giving the government greater powers to monitor civilians in the name of 'security' and 'public interest'. For instance, there exists no uniform national policy to regulate public CCTV coverage. Different departments and institutions such as the police, municipal administrations, railway authorities, and residential welfare associations may adopt their own internal practices without undertaking any effort to harmonize their information management processes or adhere to any rigorous data protection measures. In 2018, the Ministry of Home Affairs used the powers conferred by Section 69 of the IT Act, 2000 to authorize 10 government agencies to intercept, monitor and decrypt 'any information generated, transmitted, received or

---

[43]https://www.businesstoday.in/current/economy-politics/aadhaar-data-breach-details-leak-google-search-uidai-mera-aadhaar-meri-pehchan/story/272936.html

[44]https://www.firstpost.com/tech/news-analysis/aadhaar-database-access-found-to-be-sold-on-whatsapp-for-rs-500-uidai-official-acknowledges-major-data-breach-4286427.html

stored in any computer resource'. Furthermore, the government has recently declared its intention to adopt autonomous face recognition technologies in its surveillance network in a bid to fight crime.[45] The liberal use of Internet blackouts by the administration to curb unrest or control the spread of 'rumours' is equally concerning from a privacy perspective, as cutting civilians off from their means of accessing the banking network or from conducting any business to earn a livelihood, directly affects their personal autonomy. In fact, India leads the world in Internet shutdowns[46] and it is estimated that the country lost $985 million to Internet shutdowns in 2015.[47] While ensuring the safety of its people must indeed be a priority of the state, it is alarming that none of these proposals or recommendations pay any heed to personal autonomy or privacy.

The executive oft-times makes no pretenses of violating even firmly established legal norms of liberty and privacy. A well-publicized example of this is the infamous PUBG incident in Rajkot, Gujarat, where the police arrested 10 students for playing a video game which the local administration and state police had decided to ban without having the authority to do so.[48] Perhaps just as concerning as government authorities' lack of respect for individual privacy in direct contradiction

---

[45]https://indianexpress.com/article/explained/automated-facial-recognition-what-ncrb-proposes-what-are-the-concerns-5823110/

[46]https://www.newamerica.org/weekly/edition-244/creeping-rise-internet-shutdowns-india/

[47]https://www.brookings.edu/wp-content/uploads/2016/10/intenet-shutdowns-v-3.pdf

[48]https://timesofindia.indiatimes.com/gadgets-news/pubg-ban-in-a-first-for-india-10-college-students-arrested-for-playing-pubg-mobile/articleshow/68406376.cms

to judgments of the highest court, is the interaction of state agencies with technology companies that collect and process user data. For instance, the CBI violated international standards by asking social media companies to use Microsoft's Photo DNA software—a technology that computationally identifies images, audio and video using hash values—to aid in its criminal investigations. Due to the high risk of misuse, the software is typically used by social media giants only to help with investigations into child exploitation. The CBI, unfortunately, gave no such formal reassurance.[49] A collusion between the government and social media giants would be a cause for great alarm and spell the death knell for democracy as we know it. The judiciary will have to take centre stage in ensuring that such dangerous situations are nipped in the bud. The courts of this country will be required to take a more proactive stand in safeguarding individuals from powerful entities with the ability to misuse their data. The Supreme Court, especially, will have the crucial task of ensuring that standards and guidelines are put in place if the legislature shirks its responsibility.

The Supreme Court has demonstrated an exceptional degree of nuance in the past when it comes to balancing privacy with the interests of public administration. It will be required to demonstrate more of this skilful nuance in the years to come.

---

[49]https://www.indiatoday.in/magazine/up-front/story/20190114-right-to-privacy-one-fell-snoop-1422361-2019-01-04

25

NEW CHALLENGES FOR THE SUPREME COURT: THE COVID CRISIS

Reports started emerging in late 2019 of a new, contagious flu-like disease in the Chinese city of Wuhan. The virus was a mutation of the SARS virus that had killed hundreds of thousands of people around the world from 2002–2004, and it was allegedly born in the live animal wet markets of Wuhan. However, it became clear, very quickly, that this virus—named COVID-19 was exponentially more severe than the earlier strains of the SARS virus—both in terms of contagiousness and fatality. The coronavirus possesses an incubation period of upto two weeks and the symptoms are largely indistinguishable from the mild seasonal flu. This, coupled with the Chinese Government's negligence in containing the disease and instead attempting to cover up its existence, allowed the virus to spread to all corners of the globe through international travel. The coronavirus soon devastated Europe, made its inroads into North America, and eventually entered India. The Government of India was initially caught off-guard and dallied in its response. However, it soon became clear that mere airport screening was not an adequate response and that strict measures would have to be taken rapidly in order to protect a billion-strong population afflicted with widespread poverty.

While the government was obliviously drawing up plans for some semblance of a pandemic-response strategy, the Indian Bar and Judiciary had the foresight to realize the severity of the virus as well as the challenges that it will have to address, regardless of the government's decisions. It was recognized that the physical infrastructure of the national court system was not designed to accommodate the overwhelming crowd that gathers in its establishments on a daily basis. From the most humble of rural magistrate's courts to the Supreme Court itself, courtrooms are often tightly packed with lawyers, clerks and litigants. Most lawyers' chambers are small and stifling; and the premises of every court are teeming with salesmen, contractors, litigants, and ordinary laymen. Various members of the legal fraternity were self-aware enough to understand that the courts were a high-risk zone for viral transmission—a single person carrying such an infectious pathogen could put hundreds of people at risk. Various high courts around the country developed protocols to be followed by themselves and all subordinate courts, adjourning all matters except urgent ones and cutting down on the presence of court staff. The Bar Council of India, similarly, issued instructions to all State Bar Councils to start shutting down their offices. While slower to respond than several high courts, the Supreme Court started thermal screening at the premises entrance, enforcing social distancing norms and decongesting its section offices by giving three-day holidays to staff in two rotations. However, it took various petitions from bar associations as well as impending state and national lockdowns to incentivize the Supreme Court to consider a total shutdown of the court premises and rely on technological solutions to ensure that it fulfilled its role of justice delivery. Meetings between members of the bar and bench were successful, leading to the Supreme Court passing an order directing all courts across the nation to adopt e-filing and virtual hearing procedures in order to retain limited functioning during the pendency of the national lockdown. While the high courts were entrusted with looking after their states and formulating rules for all district courts under their supervision, the Supreme Court laid down norms for its own hearings.

The Court ordered that mentioning for all urgent matters would be directed towards the Registrar, that all petitions would be filed electronically and hearings would be conducted through video conferencing. While in principle such resolutions seemed straightforward, in practice the Court had to undergo numerous stages of trial-and-error. For instance, one of the earliest implementations of virtual hearings involved setting up a special teleconferencing room inside the Supreme Court where an advocate would have to arrive personally and speak to the bench which was sitting in a separate chamber. While no doubt this policy would have minimized exposure of the judges, it was doing nothing to alleviate the risk faced by lawyers and their colleagues who would have to leave their residence and arrive at the Supreme Court in person anyway. It was only after further petitioning (and the complete shutdown of public transport and lawyers' chambers) that the Court set up an online infrastructure by which advocates could enter appearances from their home offices.

Of course, having a purely online system also brought

its own share of challenges. Most lawyers, unfamiliar with technology, were having a hard time adapting to alien procedures. There were routine complaints that glitches or technical issues were compromising the quality of advocacy or the judges' appreciation of arguments, with no established protocols to immediately redress such concerns. While it is likely that some critics of the online system were looking for an easy scapegoat for their own poor performance, there is no denying that the technological unfamiliarity of several stakeholders has been brought about by the fact that the judiciary and legal profession in general has for long viewed technological adoption as an interesting academic topic rather than a pressing practical need. Indeed, the Bar Council of India eventually petitioned the Supreme Court to start allowing physical hearings because 90 per cent of advocates and judges across the country were allegedly unable to come to grips with the nuances of the technology. While certain fora such as the National Green Tribunal have been at the forefront of adopting paperless and e-hearing procedures, there exist no continuing legal education initiatives that will incentivize the legal profession to stay up-to-date with modern technology. The Supreme Court also resisted a golden opportunity to begin a new chapter in transparency and accountability by refusing to permit live webcasting of judicial proceedings. While it is unfortunate that it took a global health crisis to belatedly motivate the Supreme Court to improve its dated procedures, it is nonetheless a welcome move, as the Court announced that virtual courts were here to stay.

The Supreme Court through this pandemic has clearly demonstrated that virtual courts are equally capable of ensuring justice for the poor and the marginalized. Initially, the Court was slow in recognizing the tragedy and plight of the unorganized labour sector caused by the sudden announcement of lockdown. People, in lakhs, having lost faith in the capabilities of the administrative institutions to safeguard their right to life and well-being, started walking a long journey back home and several lives were lost in the process.

The Supreme Court took *suo moto* cognizance of the migrant labour crisis during the lockdown and after wide coverage by the media. The entire labour population suddenly found themselves out of work and were confined to their small rooms, often shared by five or six other labourers. On a normal day, their rooms were just a place to sleep. But now, without work and without income, the people suddenly fell into a state of panic and confusion, whilst scores of others went hungry. Shelters and NGOs saw lines, stretching several kilometers, of people waiting for food. Some would join the line in the morning and reach the head of the line in time for dinner.

Frustrated and realizing that there were no measures in place for their security and well-being, millions of labourers in the cities, gathered at bus terminals and train stations, with hopes of finding transport back to their villages. During the month of March, the labourers had seen several news reports of the government airlifting and evacuating people from the Covid hit countries. They had genuinely expected some sort of arrangement for themselves as well. However, all they received was a lathi charge and other coercive measures to go back to their confinements.

Finally taking cognizance of the matter, the Supreme Court had passed a slew of directions to the government to ensure that the labourers were given proper food and shelter. As the lockdown progressed, the Supreme Court had passed directions to ensure that transportation for the labourers was provided free of charge. During the final stages of the lockdown, the Supreme Court directed the state governments and union territories to conduct skill-mapping of the returned labourers at the village and district, and develop employment mechanisms for them. The Central Government was also directed to widely circulate its rehabilitation schemes so that the migrant workers could duly avail them.

In the final analysis, the Supreme Court and the other high courts in the country ensured that the poorest and the marginalized got some relief in terms of their well-being.

EPILOGUE

Courts have been generally perceived as institutions capable of objectively determining right and wrong and removing opinion from this process, which is accentuated by the fact that judges are merely expected to apply the laws to the circumstance and accordingly pass judgment.

However, as we explored and came to understand more about these institutions, we found that delivering judgment was neither easy nor clear. As we climbed up the hierarchy of courts and examined the types and nature of issues presented before the Supreme Court, we realized that law is not all that clear, and the notional principles of morality and justiciability guide the judges in dispensing justice. It is as much a philosophical process as it is a practical one.

Principles of morality vary significantly across societies and religions, but they are all underpinned by a common foundation—the Golden Rule:

> Avoid doing what you would blame others for doing.
>
> —*Thales of Miletus*

> What is hateful to you, do not do to your fellow: this is the whole Torah; the rest is the explanation.
>
> —*Babylonian Talmud*

> If the entire Dharma can be said in a few words, then it is—that which is unfavourable to us, do not do that to others.
>
> —*Padma Purana*

> Zigong asked, 'Is there any one word that could guide a person throughout life?' The Master replied, 'How about reciprocity: never impose on others what you would not choose for yourself?'
>
> —*The Analects*

The principle is basically to treat others how you wish to be treated. It is beautifully apt in the justice delivery system, but extremely difficult to objectively apply. It is the principle of reciprocity. It demands of the person sitting in judgment to be able to visualize and empathize with the situation and then determine the appropriate action. Needless to say, it is a demanding task.

If the Constitution remained today the same as when it began—a seemingly abstract, dry and fanciful collection of words and phrases, it would not have held much importance. But the history of independent India expressed through judicial dynamism reveals the actualization of the words written in the Constitution.

It has weathered the test of time, and the Supreme Court

has been able to guard the spirit of the Constitution. Its successes are reflected through the progress and advancement of society.

A country once divided and torn, separated by language, religion and culture, now stands united. It stands as the largest and most successful democracy in the world.

The judges with their progressive forethought are perhaps, no less than oracles. They set the wheels in motion—for progress. Only the future will tell us whether the Supreme Court has been successful in tackling the new socio-cultural challenges of the twenty-first century. One thing is for certain—the jurisprudential trajectory of the nation has entered a new orbit. All eyes will remain affixed on the Supreme Court to see how it runs with its role as the custodian of the basic structure of the Constitution.

So aptly, we may remember the words of two great Americans, who expressed similar sentiments, nearly a century apart from each other:

Thomas Jefferson, on 28 September 1820:

> 'I know no safe depository of the ultimate powers of the society but the people themselves; and if we think them not enlightened enough to exercise their control with a wholesome discretion, the remedy is not to take it from them, but to inform their discretion by education. This is the true corrective of abuses of constitutional power...'
>
> —Thomas Jefferson, letters of Thomas Jefferson

Justice Louis D. Brandeis on 5 July 1915:

> 'Our form of government, as well as humanity, compels us to strive for the development of the individual man. Under universal suffrage (soon to be extended to women) every voter is a partner of the State. Unless the rulers have, in the main, education and character and are free men, our great experiment in democracy must fail...'
>
> —Justice Louis D. Brandeis in *True Americanism*

Both these cardinal thoughts find a unique resonance in our Constituent Assembly in the person of Dr B.R. Ambedkar who very prophetically observed:

> 'I shall not therefore enter into the merits of the Constitution. Because I feel, however good a Constitution may be, it is sure to turn out bad because those who are called to work it, happen to be a bad lot. However bad a Constitution may be, it may turn out to be good if those who are called to work it, happen to be a good lot. The working of a Constitution does not depend wholly upon the nature of the Constitution. The Constitution can provide only the organs of State such as the Legislature, the Executive and the Judiciary. The factors on which the working of those organs of the State depend are the people and the political parties they will set up as their instruments to carry out their wishes and their politics...'
>
> —Dr B.R. Ambedkar on 25 November 1949 in the Constituent Assembly

ACKNOWLEDGEMENTS

My deepest gratitude to my team of advocates comprising Aniruddha Purushotham, Manoranjan Paikaray, Satyabrata Panda and Abeer Sharma. They devoted their precious time and energy to make this book possible.

INDEX